Think and *Speak* Like God

RESTORING

Mankind's True Identity

By Geovanni I. Guerra

O.T.W.
PUBLISHING INC.

References used throughout the book are as follows:

Bible quotes taken from the King James Version (Public domain due to age) Definitions sourced from, partially sourced from, or paraphrased from:

American Dictionary of the English Language, Noah Webster, 1828, Facsimile First Edition. Permission to reprint the 1828 edition granted by
G. & C. Merriam Company copyright © 1967 & 1995 (renewal) by Rosalie
J. Slater, Published by the Foundation for American Christian Education
P.O. Box 27035, San Francisco, California 94127

When referencing the Strong Concordance, the word Strong was used.

Projects, Contributors to Wikimedia. "Strong's Exhaustive Concordance of the Bible (1890) by James Strong." Wikisource, the Free Online Library, Wikimedia Foundation, Inc., 25 Feb. 2021, en.m.wikisource.org/wiki/ Strong%27s_Exhaustive_Concordance. This work was published before January 1, 1926, and is in the public domain worldwide because the author died at least 100 years ago.

Published by:
Overcoming The World Publishing, Inc., Chicago, IL.

Email: **overcomingtheworldpublishing@gmail.com**
For speaking engagements, email: **israelgeovanniguerra@gmail.com**
Cover by LawrenceCampbell.com
Email: ContactMe@LawrenceCampbell.com

TABLE OF CONTENTS

Chapter Six

Chapter Seven

ACKNOWLEDGMENTS

I would like to give all glory and honor to God, who took me out of the darkness and brought me into the Kingdom of Light through Jesus Christ. Without Jesus, I would not have been restored to this beautiful journey of ruling and reigning in life by the power of His Word. To the divine third person of the Trinity, the Holy Spirit, who is the Ultimate Teacher of the Church and all members in it that gain divine revelation, of which none of us would be able to understand the mysteries of the Kingdom of God, if it weren't for Him.

I also want to thank my wife, Elsy O. Guerra, for her love and support. My children, for their continual love toward me, I am truly blessed to be your father. Thanks to my mother, Ivonne P. Munoz, for praying for me when I was out in the world and my family for all their support.

I want to thank all the mentors, spiritual leaders, and instructors God placed in my life to teach me sound doctrine and encourage me to keep walking by faith. The early believers in the Church of Jesus Christ from the first century to the present, for the times they yielded to the Holy Spirit, allowing for the sound doctrine of Christ our Lord to be taught. Despite the Church's history, which is composed of believers who often responded out of carnality and not the Spirit, this has caused great harm. Still, the mercy of the Lord allowed many of the same believers to, at times, operate out of the Holy Spirit to preserve His Church as they operated in Faith. God demonstrates the grace He has given through the merits of Jesus Christ alone to those who believe in the perfect work of the Cross. Furthermore, it is more than enough for fallen humanity to turn away from sin and turn to God in faith to be saved if they choose it.

To Jhan Moskowitz, my dear friend, who delights in the presence of the Lord. Thank you for taking the time to pour into my life through bible studies and special times of conversations and direct impartation by the Spirit of God, leading us.

To Pastor Bill Winston for being used of the Holy Spirit to teach the incorruptible Word of God without compromise, which has confirmed and edified my life to the glory of God. To Kenneth E. Hagin, who is in the presence of the Lord, for the teachings on faith that the Holy Spirit gifted him to deliver to edify the body of Christ. To Bishop Christopher Lewis, thank you for being a true friend and brother. To the board of World Wide Ministry 4 Yeshua Inc., Saul Santos, and Jorge Medina, your support enabled me to move forward with God's Vision and plan for my life.

Thank you to everyone who helped by leading me through making this book a reality. I made every effort to put together what God has taught me throughout my walk with Him to be a blessing to the body of Christ. The revelation in this book is composed of the things God has taught me in my prayer time, studying His Word, and throughout the many people God has used to confirm through the anointing how to be a doer of the Word of God by faith, rooted in love. Nevertheless, I cannot say I have not made mistakes along the way. The first edition of this book came out in 2015, and there were a lot of grammar errors, formatting errors, and even citing sources the correct way. I hope these errors have been corrected in this version. Still, if there are some minor errors, please note that this book is not written in the form of academic writing, although it has been researched to be used as a solid source. Instead, it is a powerful-Holy-Spirit-filled tool that the Holy Spirit will guide you through as the teacher of the Church. May God bless all who read this book abundantly. May the revelation of God's Word empower all to a 100% Victory by faith in Christ Jesus. Amen!

Foreword

"Author and Minister Geovanni Guerra is a brother, friend, and co-laborer with me in the building and the advancement of God's Kingdom. His heart for God and his passion to globally advance the Kingdom of God are contagious, which you will agree with after having read this book. *Think and Speak Like God Restoring Mankind's True Identity* not only contains a lifetime of principles cultivated from biblical-theological truths but also a practical life lesson."

Bishop Christopher A. Lewis
Christian Community Church of God
Lauderhill, FL

Foreword

"Mental transformation starts with the words of your mouth. "*Think and Speak Like God Restoring Mankind's True Identity*" is such an awesome read, and the spirit of this book speaks victory to the reader. It shows us that the way to overcome the enemy is in the mind, one of the essential areas of the believer's life. It further explains that the Word of God does both the exposing of the mind and the repairing of it. In-depth, this book speaks great truth regarding the role of perversion against the mind and the dangers of double-mindedness. The content of Think and Speak Like God Restoring Mankind's True Identity explains the powerful use of imagination and provides great instruction in showing the reader how to biblically restore their mind. There is no doubt that the author did a great deal of study, prayer, and consideration to obtain such a revelation. Everybody should have a copy of this book to learn how much the Bible has to say about the mind, imagination, and the words we speak."

Dr. Norman Thomas, Jr.
New Life Church International
Lake Charles, LA

Holy Spirit Inspired Quotes

"The most effective way to love anyone is by dying to your selfishness for their gain. Of course, this action does not guarantee they will appreciate it or love you in return. Nevertheless, the action to love unselfishly is what true love is really about, and it is the reason why God sent His Son, Jesus Christ, to demonstrate His true love for the whole world."

"Without God, humanity interprets lust to equal love and therefore ends up heartbroken, for they do not know God who is love."

"To find the most precious gems, such as diamonds, you must be willing to dig deeper than finding the more common gems. Unfortunately, in today's society, not too many people are willing to explore deeply to find the true treasures of life. We must awaken to the privilege God gives us to dig deep into His Word and history to find precious gems He has left for us to discover."

"Do not be surprised when you are genuinely reaching out in God's love, that almost all the time, people will be suspicious of your intent. You have to realize the carnal mind has so many under its influence that they are not used to the authentic love of God with no strings attached. Yet, we are to love all."

"Lack of communication and suspicion are weapons of the enemy to keep the body of Christ from understanding how to flow in unity. That, and the inability of many who refuse to think that perhaps they don't know everything. Saints, we must remain teachable to all Holy Spirit-filled teachings."

"Two things that look the same in the natural realm but are very different in the spiritual realm are tolerance and long-suffering. Tolerance will put up with someone based on the circumstances, yet its root is carnal. Long-suffering endures in love and willfully lays down its life for the benefit of another."

INTRODUCTION

This book contains revelation and understanding often missed by many who long for results that God Himself obtains through the power of His Word. By the time you finish reading this book, you will no longer walk in defeat as you allow the Holy Spirit of God to bring forth the revelation through the Grace of our Lord, Jesus Christ. Furthermore, as you apply the revelation that God gives you to every circumstance and situation you face, you will walk in the fullness of the Word of the Living God.

Before you go any further, you must understand that Chapters One and Two are designed to lay the foundation. Therefore, please make sure not to skip them, as they are essential to rightly divide the Word of God and ensure that you receive sound doctrine according to the Word of God. Once the proper foundation and understanding of how God made humanity is established, one can begin the beautiful journey of hope, faith, and love. A journey where you can hear from God, think with His mind, speak His words, and manifest His will into existence. Finally, one can receive everything God has promised to those who have been restored to His image through Jesus Christ, whose original Hebrew name is Y'shua Hamashiach. (Pronounced "Yeh-shoo-ah.")

For those who have not received Jesus as their Lord and Savior, I would ask that you take a moment to open your heart and mind to receive all that God will communicate to you as you read things that you may have never heard before. For instance, in **Genesis 1:1-2**, God created the heavens and the earth. God is Eternal, and He operates outside of time and in time. What may be interpreted as thousands, millions, or billions of years by humanity in the past was an attempt to explain and communicate natural time. However, we must remember that to God, one day can be a billion years, and a billion years can be as one day (see **2 Peter 3:8**). The Bible was written thousands of years ago, the Old Testament was written before Jesus Christ came, and the New Testament was written after the death and resurrection of Christ. As a result, the language and vocabulary used in the Bible were not as developed as today in the twenty-first century. For example, the word *billion* did not appear until about the 16th century, long after the Bible was written. Another example in the Bible would be the word *unicorn*, be it a single horn unicorn or double horn unicorn, which refers to what we know as the rhinoceros and not some mythical creature as some have ignorantly assigned to the Bible. Also, it is essential to note that the word *earth* in the Bible does not just refer to our planet but can also refer to any form of visible terrestrial matter, which includes every planet in the universe, even though for a long time, humanity, out of ignorance, has used it to mean only our planet.

Furthermore, many things described in the Bible that seem awkward in description only solidify the point that the vocabulary was limited at the time. For example, to explain to people thousands of years ago what a car with lights carrying people looked like, the prophet's limited vocabulary could, at best, perhaps say it was a chariot of fire. Other times, the mysterious description communicates a divine message from God, such as the descriptions of particular creatures in the Bible. There are many more examples in the Bible that one will come across as you read it that will stop some people from studying it further due to a misunderstanding of how they interpret what was written. Reading something in its proper context can help clarify many misconceptions and help gain a perspective that will enrich a person's life with an open heart and mind.

Moreover, most people would agree that it would be a double standard for people to accept the so-called scientific explanation of dark matter as something not visible yet taken into account. Or a black hole that you can see its effect on objects that draw close enough to it in space. And reject that similarly, that explanation applies to that which is spiritual. You can see the effect of spiritual forces on people depending on which one they draw close to, even if they are nonbelievers. For example, if people are of God, they are inspired by God, who is invisible, and you can clearly see the effect through those who obey God and bring forth what is good. On the contrary, you can see the invisible inspiration of evil upon humanity who reject God and obey the evil impulses that lead their lives to steal, kill, pervert, lust, enslave, and abuse others.

In the same way, one can see the effect of the wind moving a leaf or feel the wind blowing. Still, the wind itself is not visible, in the same way God is seen, by the effect of His first initiation of life upon all living things that are granted His mercy, be it people that are just or unjust. So, a person who knew me before receiving Christ can testify to having observed my life before Christ Jesus and witnessed the void and emptiness in it. Conversely, one can see my life with Christ now and see His life and provision with an abundance of good things to show for it. Furthermore, suppose science requires observable facts to prove its findings. In that case, the lives of those born again in spirit by God are full of observable proof, as well as the lives of those under the influence of other spiritual forces that lead to confusion, chaos, and emptiness.

I truly believe that all people who are open-minded to all that is written in this book will, at the minimum, gain a perspective that will help enrich their lives for the better. And at best, they will encounter the living God, to which their lives will never be the same as they experience who Love is and develop their own relationship with God. May God bless you in Christ Jesus' name, amen.

Next, for believers in Jesus Christ, it is crucial to identify that there is an inheritance that the Church received of God by the Spirit through Jesus Christ, and an inheritance that the church structures and organizations created by men and women who often operated carnally also passed down to the churches. In recognizing the difference between the inheritance of the saints by the Spirit and that which the churches have inherited through the carnal decisions of the church, one can gain an understanding to let go of the carnal practices that are not of the Spirit of the Lord.

Firstly, the Church must accept the fact that carnality has influenced many of the decisions that were made in the history of the Church. From the first century, after the holy apostles of the lamb transitioned to be present with the Lord, those who continued in the Faith did the best they knew how, yet many times yielded to the social pressures and went against the authentic teachings of Christ, which resulted in a carnal church. Nevertheless, leaders in the Church such as Justin Martyr, Irenaeus, and Tertullian in the second and third centuries, Augustine of Hippo from the fourth century, Maximus of Constantinople in the seventh century, Anselm of Canterbury in the eleventh to twelfth century, Martin Luther in the sixteenth century. Friedrich Schleiermacher, Soren Kierkegaard, John Henry Newman in the nineteenth century, to Charles Spurgeon, D.L. Moody, Maria Woodworth-Etter, Smith Wigglesworth, E.W. Kenyon, John G. Lakes, A.W. Tozer, and others all operated like all other believers who are seeking God and having to deal with the social pressures and teachings of their time. These leaders of the church in history mentioned from the first century to the twentieth century all at times operated out of carnality and other times out of the Spirit. At some point in history, the church stopped teaching in line with the doctrines of Christ that demonstrated the gospel of the Kingdom of God preached with power, signs, and wonders, and inherited teachings that were of humanity's understanding. Still, at other times, the super-intelligence of God illuminated church leaders and other believers in Christ Jesus. Still, most of the church's history has unfortunately been of a carnal understanding.

Furthermore, the structures that now form many things in the churches are rooted in carnality. Nevertheless, God, through the Spirit, has graced us to obtain that which is of Him as our inheritance, which He has given us in Christ by way of the Holy Spirit. The decision the Church must make in our time of understanding what took place in the History of the Church is to receive that which is of the Spirit of the Lord and get rid of what the carnal church established and passed down throughout the centuries. By forsaking the ways of the carnal church, the Spirit Church of Christ can begin to build and establish the authenticity of what the Church has inherited in the Spirit and begin to reflect the beauty of the Lord to a world that is in panic and confusion by ways of pandemics, and divisions of all sorts caused by sin that entered the world when humanity disobeyed God's command in the garden of Eden.

Without a doubt, to get rid of all the mistakes of the carnal church that have been passed down from generation to generation is easier said than done. However, it is a choice each member of the body of Christ must make. This book, which God has graced me to share with you, *"Think and Speak Like God Restoring Mankind's True Identity,"* is designed to show you who God has made you so that you may know your true identity and gain insight into the inexhaustible inheritance all believers have by way of the Holy Spirit through the merits of Christ Jesus our Lord.

Finally, one would benefit most from this book's revelation by spending some time in worship and prayer before opening this book and reading from it. Worshipping God and praying will help prepare you to receive all the Holy Spirit desires to reveal and impart as your inheritance as a child of God. Remember that Jesus Christ died on the cross and paid the price for the sin of the world. As one repents and believes in Him, He accounts His perfect righteousness as our own through the blood that He shed to remit our sins and rose again for our justification. HalleluYah!

A picture of maturity in Christ is far beyond just healing and gifts of the Spirit. Gifts of the Spirit are available for all who yield to the Holy Spirit, though we do not undermine them, for they are amazing. A true sign of maturity as a son of God is total obedience to God the Father. It is the ability to love those who will talk behind your back, not realizing that the Holy Spirit has let you in on the murmuring of their hearts. Yet, instead of lashing out at them, you love them and are willing to die to yourself for their sake so that they might repent and see that the one they are rejecting, mocking, and judging is not you but the One who sent you. The One who abides in you, with whom you have become one. You see, the true sign of maturity is laying down your life for the benefit of the other. Are you willing to die for that stranger to be saved? Don't be quick to answer that, be honest. To mature is a process that can be instantaneous or gradual, and that is between you and God. Yet God's love is so amazing that you are covered either way as you have embraced Jesus Christ-Y'shua the Messiah as your Lord! Shalom!

O pinions that are opposite to the Absolute Truth will always be offended by it. Those who believe their lies to be true when faced with the Absolute Truth will either be offended and reject God, who is that Absolute Truth, or humble themselves and repent of their opposition to the Absolute Truth.

G od sees your heart; remember that, people. God knows who he has made you in Christ Jesus. He knows your intentions and motives because if you are in the body of Christ Jesus, He put them there. So do not worry about it when you are misunderstood or judged by others. Jesus was misunderstood and judged by others, but notice His heart expressed on the cross, "Father forgive them for they know not what they do" (Luke 23:34). The enemy will try to get people to judge you, but don't let it bother you, overcome his evil with good and love all people.

"Restoring Mankind's True Identity"

CHAPTER ONE

Man (Male/Female), made in the Image of God

T he undeniable reality is that humanity is a mystery of invisible and visible substances: spirit, soul, and body. God, who is Spirit, grants understanding to those who seek Him in Spirit and Truth through Jesus Christ, the Spirit Word of God incarnated as a man, although he was God, to show us the way.

Man, Made in The Image Of God

There is a uniqueness that God made each individual with the potential to display a dimension of His love in a manner that only that person can express. We are one of a kind to the degree that once God made us, He broke the mold. This reason alone should be enough to move all who profess to love God to desire every person on the earth to get saved. For in people being saved and restored to God, their enablement and potential to display Jesus's love visibly in the world is made available. Just think about this: our first love, Jesus Christ, is inexhaustible. A beauty and feature of God's love can come out of every person made in His image and likeness.

Furthermore, the King James Version of the Bible states:

> And God said, Let us make man in our image, after our likeness: and let them have dominion over the fish of the sea, and over the fowl of the air, and over the cattle, and over all the earth, and over every creeping thing that creepeth upon the earth. **So God created man in his own image, in the image of God created he him; male and female created he them. 28 And God blessed them, and God said unto them, Be fruitful, and multiply, and replenish the earth, and subdue it: and have dominion over the fish of the sea, and over the fowl of the air, and over every living thing that moveth upon the earth. (Genesis 1:26-28)**

From the very beginning, we find that God made man in His image and His likeness. The word *"image"* means _to render visible: resemblance_. The word *"likeness"* means _similarity in appearance or character or nature between two things or persons_. That is why the Word of God says of Jesus Christ, the second and last type of man that He is the image of the invisible God **(see Colossians 1:15)**. That should thrill you if you know precisely what God's agenda is for humanity. Look closely at God's original intent for humankind, whom He has restored through Jesus Christ, as we accept Him. We find that God initially made man (male and female) to express His image, nature, and influence upon the visible earth realm.

As we see in **Genesis 1:26-28**, God gave humanity all power and authority over the earth. **God was to be the only source for man.** God made the earth and blessed man and put him upon it to be fruitful, to multiply, to replenish the earth, and literally make the earth "*as it is in Heaven*."

The man(male and female) was to subdue the earth, meaning it would be under his control. This authority was given to him so that things that needed to be ordered and put in their proper place would be. Man's dominion on the earth was to continue by the inspiration of God. Overall, God wanted Heaven duplicated on Earth so that man could lord over it, and God could come and fellowship with man on Earth. Therefore, man could enjoy an eternal friendship with God, having life, abundance, and peace. However, when the time came for man to subdue the serpent that Satan used, he did not. Man failed to obey God's instruction not to partake of the tree of knowledge of good and evil (see **Genesis 2:16-17**). Instead, he chose to spectate and not dominate.

One can say that man took his woman and used her as a guinea pig to see if death would overcome her, as God said it would, or if, for some strange reason, God was holding something back from him. When the man saw that his mate did not die a physical death, he partook of the forbidden fruit that looked good and ripe for eating.

He ate the forbidden fruit that would give the man and woman the knowledge of good and evil, for it was not God's desire for mankind to know evil. Humanity soon discovered that they were naked, for the glory and spirit with which God had dressed them departed because of their disobedience. Humanity would have to rely on a perverted knowledge of the source they decided to partake of, that source's root being Satan, the father of lies. Humanity would not have the ability to recognize the truth that God had been providing to them. Their new nature of sin now blinded them. This sinful nature hid them from knowing God, though He was always present (see **Isaiah 59:1-2**).

Consequently, humanity, who believed the serpent's lie, was left to their senses, processing information without the undistorted communion of the Spirit of Truth to guide them. Evil and fear kept Mankind blind and in doubt of the absolute truth given by God. At this point, man's journey began in a fallen state in which his new god (Satan) would bring about his nature: death, void, and darkness. In an attempt to imitate the one true God, Satan began to inspire humanity to create a world in which he, Satan, would be a god. A world where men suffer the curse of toiling and sweating. Humanity would build itself a world that resembled Satan, producing jealousy and envy with so much evil that men began to murder each other, even among brothers.

In all that, God had a plan for man if he missed the mark and went against His instructions. He quickly showed His man mercy and love by clothing him in animal skin, which was the only thing He could dress him in at the time. As a result, this covering caused the bloodshed of an animal that mirrors the prophecy about the covenant that God would bring about through the blood of His Holy Lamb. Oh, the great love that God has for humanity in that He did not seal the fate of humanity by condemning us to eternal death and a lake of fire.

Instead, God had His only begotten Son, Jesus, take the form of a man to restore humanity to his Creator and establish once again an intimate relationship between them. Now, through the perfect work of Jesus Christ on the Cross.

Jesus took upon Himself the sin of the world and suffered what we should have suffered. Now, all humanity has the choice to be restored to God or continue in darkness (see **John 3:16-17; II Corinthians 5:21; Romans 5:17**).

Those who received Jesus Christ (Y'shua the Messiah) as their Lord and Savior once again have access to do the will of God on earth, as it is in Heaven. The blessing of the Lord has been restored. However, those who have not accepted God's gift and the forgiveness of sin continue under the god of this world system (Satan), which continues to abuse and leave them void of life. Although Satan has established a system in this world that appears to have life, it always leads to emptiness and not being fulfilled (see **Matthew 16:26**). Unfortunately, some of humanity lose their souls and suffer an unnecessary fate: a lake of fire and eternal damnation.

A Time to Reflect

I want you to think about every mistake you have ever made. Every problem you have ever caused yourself or those around you. What if God offered to erase all your failures and mistakes as though they never took place before Him? What if He said, I will erase from My knowledge every account and record that proves you were at fault and wipe it out before Me as though it had never existed? Sounds too good to be true, right? Well, it is too good, and it is the absolute truth.

God dealt with sin for all humankind. However, people are not aware of this gift. As a result, many go on suffering in this world and, even worse, for all eternity. God has already made available to everyone to be in right standing with Him and receive His blessing upon their lives and everything they touch. However, He will never force them to receive it. He simply extends this gift of love to all who will receive it from Him.

I would like to take a moment and ask for the patience of my brothers and sisters, who are born again and have access to all that God has given us through Jesus Christ. I request this intermission to speak to those who have not accepted Jesus Christ as their Lord and Savior. You see, to think and speak like God and achieve complete victory, you must be born of His Spirit. Victory only happens by believing that God sent His Son, Jesus Christ (Y'shua Messiah), to die for the world's sins. Jesus was buried, and after the 3rd day, He was raised from the dead by the Holy Spirit. By Jesus, we have been justified before the One True Holy God. Jesus paid the price for our sin, and we can now be counted in right standing with God because He is our advocate. He paid the price for our justification even though we were guilty as charged (see **Romans 3:23; 10:8-11; John 3:16-17**). If you are ready for the gift of salvation, believe in your heart and confess with your mouth the following confession of faith.

Say: *"God, I confess Jesus Christ, who took the sin of the world, mine included, suffered and paid the punishment of death (which I deserved) as my Lord and Savior. I receive the gift of God, which I cannot earn by good deeds, but because I believe that Jesus Christ is the Son of God who died and rose on the third day by the power of the Holy Spirit and is now at your right hand. God, I accept this gift from Your undeserving favor toward me, and I thank You that I am restored unto You. I am now a new creature, a child of Yours, God, who will bring about Your will on earth as it is in Heaven. You teach me, and I will share your good news with all whom I am to lead. Fill me now with Your Holy Spirit and power. Give me understanding and revelation of all Your benefits and gifts and the purpose You have placed for me so that I may glorify Your name. Thank You. I count it done and count all things in my past forgiven and forgotten by You. I declare that I am of light and now begin the process of renewing my mind to what is the absolute truth: Your Word. God, I declare this all in the name of my Lord and Savior, Jesus Christ, and I am in expectancy of all that You will do with me for Your glory in Jesus' name. Amen!"*

To whom it may concern: Depression is a thought given by your enemy; it is not your identity. Refuse false thoughts in Jesus' name, amen.

Before I proceed, please send an email to me at **wwm4yeshua@gmail.com** if you have just received Jesus Christ as your Lord and Savior. I ask this of you because I would like to welcome you to the Kingdom of God. I am thrilled to know that I will meet you in Heaven and that we will rule and reign for all eternity with God, who is Love. I bless you and pray, with all the love of God in me, that all God has for you begins to manifest visibly upon you, in Jesus' name, Amen!

Discovering Mankind's True Identity

In order to think like God, we must first understand who we are, for God has made us in Christ; in other words, we must know our true identity. Without an understanding of who we are. We will remain ignorant as to why God placed us on this earth and for what purpose we were created. That being said, once you receive Jesus Christ as your Lord and Savior, you are now a new creature (see **II Corinthians 5:17**). We have the same Spirit of the Lord our God, which becomes one with our Spirit. The Bible in **First Corinthians 6:17** says, *"But he that is joined unto the Lord is one spirit."* So, if you have been born again through the gift God has given through Christ Jesus, then you can say that God's Spirit is now your Spirit, and your Spirit is now God's Spirit. The vital point here is accepting Jesus as your Lord and Savior. For those who have not accepted Jesus', scripture says, *"But ye are not in the flesh, but in the Spirit, if so be that the Spirit of God dwells in you. Now, if any man has not the Spirit of Christ, he is none of his"* (**Romans 8:9**). However, this condition does not have to remain if you choose to accept Christ today.

Before we go any further, allow me to explain the components of man/woman, which are made up of **spirit, soul,** and **body. First Thessalonians 5:23** states, *"And the very God of peace sanctify you wholly; and I pray God your whole **spirit** and **soul** and **body** be preserved blameless unto the coming of our Lord Jesus Christ."* Here we see a person as a three-part being; we have a spirit, a soul, and a body. The spirit, soul, and body of a person each have a function that makes up an individual. God created man and woman this way, and we must learn from the Word of God how He designed us to operate. The only way to accomplish this is by observing the only man who fulfilled the will of God completely: Jesus, the Messiah, who teaches us for what purpose God created us upon this earth.

Thus, **the spirit of a person** is what communicates with God; it is where God becomes one with a man who has been redeemed through Jesus Christ. Here in the spirit of the redeemed man is the fullness of God, His Kingdom, His provision, His life with every spiritual blessing, and peace beyond understanding, faith, power, and miracles. All of God's abilities are in the spirit of the redeemed man. The man who has not accepted Jesus Christ as his Lord and Savior is void of God. Fallen humanity has been twisted and warped, and Satan, who is lifeless without God, is instructing them. Satan only inspires what he is: death, envy, hate, jealousy, fear, insecurity, depression, torment, and all other forms of evil.

Humanity without God though they become successful in the eyes of society according to worldly standards. Find themselves turning to drugs, alcohol, sex, suicide, the nightlife, and many other things to find some type of purpose and enjoyment. However, as Satan can only produce what he is, it leads men and women to be unsatisfied and always looking for a hint of feeling alive. Please note that I said 'feeling alive' and not 'being alive.' These are two very different things. To truly be living, you must be born of God in Spirit through Jesus Christ. Many throughout the whole earth walk deceived, thinking that they are truly alive. However, it only takes a time of reflection on each individual's account to search within themselves. To discover that, they might be moving upon the earth but walking void of fulfillment and purpose. They are deceived as to who is leading their life in the darkness and void of God. We must understand that humanity was never designed to be without God but rather to be the expression of God in this visible realm. Until humans reconnect to God, they will always seek cheap thrills that cause great spills and hurt themselves and those around them.

As for **the soul**, it is essential to know that the soul of a human is made up of the mind, will, and emotions. All humans, both the one who has been redeemed through Jesus Christ and the one who has not, have a soul. The souls of humans process the source of its information into an expression in this visible realm. If their source is light which is God, it will be processed through the soul to obtain agreement and brought into this visible realm through the body. If their source is darkness, whose root is Satan, the enemy of God, it will also be brought into this visible realm. We will go further into the different areas of the soul in the following chapters. However, for now, this will give you a foundation to build you up to think and speak like God, getting His results only through Christ Jesus.

When God gave man the authority over the earth, He caused **the Body** of man to be **the legal access for the spirit to manifest into this visible realm. This invisible source is either of light that is God or Satan's darkness, and then it is brought upon the earth through a person.** The body is made up of flesh and contains organs and senses, which are to touch, feel, smell, see, taste, and hear in the physical realm. Unfortunately, Satan has deceived the whole world into thinking that the only way something can be real and understood is through these senses.

How absurd, seeing as how humanity accepts the so-called scientific explanations of *Dark Matter,* meaning something not seen has an effect on matter that is seen. Does this sound familiar? The *Big Bang* theory, by way of a unique supernova that supposedly created everything from nothing, and we cannot forget those who believe that a type of ape gave rise to humans. All of these explanations leave humanity on paths that lead to the unknown. Many of these explanations are provided by those who do not want to accept that they are sinners who disobey God and do evil. It has gotten so bad that some highly educated people affirm that they are no different from animals. According to some of these highly educated people, only the strong will survive; therefore, it is okay to oppress weaker people and use them as they please.

Sense-based knowledge is one of the biggest lies Satan uses to keep humanity ignorant and blind. Satan manipulates people to bring about his evil will for God's creation, to hurt them, and to have them live empty lives. All of humanity is seeking God. Even atheist philosophers, whether they know it or not, are searching for peace, joy, life, and blessing. If they genuinely find it, they will be face to face with God, who is loving, kind, and merciful. God desires nothing more than to turn every area of people's lives into a place of no toil or sweat. A place like the Garden of Eden, where everything they need is in abundance.

For years, traditions of men and women have bound people to believe that they are just sinners saved by grace. That people continue to be sinners before the eyes of God even after they received Jesus Christ as their Lord and Savior, but this is incorrect. Jesus Christ paid the price of dying on the Cross and suffering the penalty of our sins so that we might now be made the righteousness of God.

II Corinthians 5:21
21 For he hath made him to be sin for us, who knew no sin; that we might be made the righteousness of God in him.

We must go to the Word of God to find our identity in Christ. When we do, we will discover the fantastic restoration of our rightful place in God's Kingdom to reign in this life by one Jesus Christ.

Romans 5:17
17 For if by one man's offence death reigned by one; much more they which receive abundance of grace and of the gift of righteousness shall reign in life by one, Jesus Christ.

This scripture in Romans 5:17 shows those of us who have become followers of Christ that it is no longer by our efforts and our ability to earn eternal life, but rather by the abundance of God's unmerited favor He poured upon us and by His gift of making us righteous. God counted what Jesus did as payment and justice for all of our past, present, and future sins. He has done that for the entire world and is waiting for those still in the world to receive what He has done for them (see **1 John 2:2**).

There is a keyword I want to focus on, as understanding this one word is essential for us to receive the manifestations of all that God has promised us in His New Covenant. That word is *FAITH.* **Hebrews 11:1** defines faith as being *"the substance of the things hoped for the evidence of things not seen."* Faith can be likened to a person who goes fishing and launches their fishing line out into the sea, specifically targeting a fish to hook and reel it in. In this case, you would target it at a promise of God's word, and by faith, you hook it and take hold of it, pulling it into the natural realm. As you develop in faith, you can exchange the fishing pole of faith for a net of faith, the size determined by your capacity to believe. You will take from the invisible realm all that you desire according to the promises of God and bring them into the visible realm. To receive all that God has provided, one must believe and have faith in what He has promised. The Word of God says, *"Without **faith**, it is impossible to please God, and those that come to Him must **believe** that He is God and that He is a rewarder of them that diligently seek him"* (see **Hebrews 11:6**).

We learn from the Gospel of Matthew that Jesus, who was continually pleasing God, in such a way that God literally opened the Heavens and with a voice testified that Jesus was His Son and He was well pleased by Him, *"And lo a voice from heaven, saying, This is my beloved Son, in whom I am well pleased,"* (**Matthew 3:17**).

I want to point out that the only thing that pleases our Father in Heaven is **faith** rooted in love brought about by hope, which He (*through Jesus Christ*) has given us. Faith is developed only to the degree that you have genuine communion with the Word of God. That implies you take time out of your day to read it, confess it, and meditate on what the Holy Spirit teaches you in this personal time of fellowship with the Word of God. I know of people who hear the Word of God, study the word of God, memorize the word of God, and still do not receive what they have studied or heard because they hear it without faith. Some people even preach the Word of God, but they do not believe it. Instead of agreeing with God's Word, they decide to say that it does not apply to this time because things have evolved into a different environment and society. However, I would never tolerate the devil's deception that continues to rob you of Heaven's best for your life.

To become a believer, you must believe that when God says, *"I have saved you,"* He has. When He says, *"I have made you of a new nature, which is good and divine,"* He has. When God says, *"I want you to live on Mount Olive, the place of rest and fruit where I will fully supply and take care of you, my ambassador on earth,"* it will be done. He simply waits for someone to believe in Him, and take of His goodness. So please make the decision today to believe God and live in Jesus' name, amen.

Indeed, after a person has repented, having realized that there are things in life beyond one's control, that person turns toward God. Depending solely on God to save them and make of them, by grace and righteousness, all that God designed them to be. Humanity can now move forward into the abundant life that Jesus Christ has provided. In **Ephesians 2:8-9** it says, *"For by grace are ye (you) saved through faith; and that not of yourselves: it is the gift of God:*

9 Not of works, least any man should boast."

GRACE, God's favor, was given to us; therefore, we could not earn it by our works. For those of us who take it by faith, it enables us to understand how God has taken us out of the darkness and translated us into the light. **Grace**, God is favoring us in such a way that He uses all of His power to work on our behalf and for our good to bring about His divine purpose for our lives in this visible earth realm. Grace says, *"I have done it all for you, and I will cause you always to triumph as you continually and solely rely on me and my promises to you."* (see **II Corinthians 2:14**).

Do you realize that He took us out of the filthy mess of bondage, waste, and sin, cleaned us up by the precious Blood of His Son Jesus Christ, that from a dunghill He moves us up to sit with Him in Heavenly places? See scriptural support below:

I Samuel 2:8
*"He raiseth up the poor out of the dust, and **lifteth up the beggar from the dunghill, to set them among princes,** and to make them inherit the throne of glory: for the pillars of the earth are the Lord's and he hath set the world upon them."*

Psalm 113:7
*"He raiseth up the poor out of the dust, and **lifteth the needy out of the dunghill.**"*

Ephesians 2:6
*"And hath **raised us up together,** and **made us sit together in heavenly places in Christ Jesus:**"*

Is this not amazing? We must meditate on what God has done for those who turn to Him. Until we understand our rightful place given to us by God Himself, who so loved us that He decided to have us reign with Him now and forever (see **Romans 8:16-18**). We will live short of God's best provision. The scriptures above exhibit God's actions. He continues to demonstrate His love for humanity by going to the filthy places of each person's life, for He is not intimidated by the foul smell of sin. God, with love, reaches into the waste places of humanity to pull them out. Having cleansed us, God repositions us into our rightful place of authority with Him.

Thus, as we are forgiven and restored to God, we must now go forth sharing the good news of the gospel of the Kingdom of God with the whole world and remember to love as Christ loved us. Therefore, never stop loving people regardless of their assumptions, regardless of their mistakes, regardless of their indifference, regardless of them looking for your fall; remember, people are not your enemy; lustful carnality is, so overcome evil with good.

To overcome evil with good, we must look to and imitate the Living Word, the Spirit made flesh—incarnated Jesus Christ. As believers in Christ, we must seek and desire to learn and do as the incarnate, resurrected Christ taught the Church to operate through the Kingdom of God on earth as it is in heaven. God's Spirit Word made flesh is what Jesus Christ was, is, did, and taught, and through each member of the body of Christ, God continues to do for His good pleasure through all that yield to Him and follow His commands that the Father in the body of Christ continue to do the works in Jesus name. Jesus-Y'shua walked in the Spirit, making visible the invisible God Father in Him, and as He did, we are now to do. To walk in the Spirit means to make the Spirit Flesh through our actions by faith in obeying God's Word as members of the body of Christ (see **Ephesians 5:30 and Galatians 5:25**).

"Restoring Mankind's True Identity"

CHAPTER TWO

As Jesus (Y'shua) is, so are we

Jesus is the Spirit Word Made Flesh, and now, as members of His body, so are we. If we, as believers in Christ, yield to Him, God the Father will continue to do the works that Jesus did and greater in His name through each one of us who co-labor with the Spirit, making Him seen to all flesh in the world.

As Jesus (Y'shua) is, so are we

First John 4:17-18 states, *Herein is our love made perfect, that we may have boldness in the day of judgment: **because as he is, so are we in this world.*** *18 There is no fear in love; but perfect love casteth out fear: because fear hath torment. He that feareth is not made perfect in love.*

Let us look at verse 17. It says here that our love is made perfect as we have boldness, confidence, and faith in the Day of Judgment. How can this be? Rest assured that Jesus Christ paid the ultimate price for the believer in Him, to have this boldness in knowing we are saved and sons of God. We are hidden in Christ Jesus as members of His body, full of God's glory and His Holy Spirit. Becoming aware of this can make some people who are under a false sense of humility uncomfortable, thinking that God may be offended or threatened if they say what He says about them. Let me assure you that God is pleased when anyone who believes in Him takes Him at His Word and manifests upon the earth as one of His sons/daughters in Christ Jesus. The end of this verse says, '*As He is, so are we in this world.*' Well! We have to find out who "*He*" is in the context of this scripture. He is God, Father, Son, and Holy Spirit, who is Love! It says here that as He is, so are we in this world! Well, how is He? Where is He? He is in Heaven, Lord of lords, King of kings, and He is without sickness or lack or poverty. He is seated upon the throne of all thrones, with His scepter fully intact, with all power and dominion. He has on His robe of righteousness, majestic, full of all wisdom and riches, strength and honor, glory and blessing (see **Revelation 5:12**).

Praise God! This thrills me. It is the absolute truth based upon the foundation of God's very Word that as believers in this earth **as He is, so are we**. The fullness of God's mercy and grace given to us through Christ Jesus has placed upon us the knowledge of what has not entered into the heart of a man without God (see **I Corinthians 2:8-10**). Nevertheless, unto us who believe that Jesus Christ-Y'shua Messiah is the Son of God. These mysteries have been given to us to know these things by the Holy Spirit of God, who is one with our Spirit (see **I Corinthians 6:17**). Therefore, by the Spirit of Revelation knowledge, I pray that you see and hear what God is saying: Please read below.

> *I have you seated with Jesus in Heavenly place* (**Ephesians 2:6**). *I have you at My table, and I do not sit My sons upon barstools or have them begging for crumbs under the table. I have you feasting at My table full of all that is of My dominion, continually instructing you and favoring you to bring upon the earth My wisdom. I give you My riches, strength, honor, and glory with blessings so that all may know I am a Living God. I have placed a crown of authority and dominion upon you, a robe of righteousness, which is My very righteousness* (**Isaiah 54:17**). *I have you sitting on a throne that I have given you, holding a scepter, powered by My scepter. I am your God, your King, and all I have; I have given through My only begotten Son Jesus Christ. You are members of My Son's body, and I see you as such: Holy, without blame and above reproach. So come boldly now saith the Spirit of the Lord, obtain mercy and grace for all the trouble that is around you to be the light and dispel all darkness and cause every lie and oppression of the devil to be eradicated by the power of the name which is above all names, the name of Jesus Christ. HalleluYah!* (**Hebrews 4:16; Colossians 1:22**)

Romans 8:16-17 says, *"The Spirit itself beareth witness with our spirit, that we are the children of God: 17And if children, then heirs; heirs of God, and joint-heirs with Christ; if so be that we suffer with him, that we may be also glorified together."* Therefore, if you have the witness of the Spirit of God and you believe that Jesus Christ is Lord of your life, this scripture is talking about you and me being heirs of God and joint-heirs with Christ. When you look at Jesus's very words, He always mentioned how all that was the Father's was His and how even the words He spoke were not His own but the Father's (see **John 14:10**).

In the same Gospels, you will find how Jesus said, *"I am in the Father, and you are in me."* Wow, you need to meditate on the Holy Scriptures and what God is saying here (see **John 10:38; 14:11-21**). God is saying to us who believe that He has restored us to our original place in Him. That is by His unmerited favor and His treatment of us in a manner far better than we deserve. God has us positioned in Christ to rule and reign for His glory and bring about His will on earth as it is in Heaven (see **Romans 5:17**).

However, we must mature as believers in order to reign in Jesus' name. Further, the word of God declares:

> Now I say, that the heir, as long as he is a child, differeth nothing from a servant, though he be lord of all; But is under tutors and governors until the time appointed of the father. Even so we, when we were children, were in bondage under the elements of the world: But when the fulness of the time was come, God sent forth his Son, made of a woman, made under the law, To redeem them that were under the law, that we might receive the adoption of sons. And because ye are sons, God hath sent forth the Spirit of his Son into your hearts, crying, Abba, Father.(**Galatians 4:1-6**)

The key here is to understand that even though we are children of God, even a child who is lord of all cannot rule from the throne until he is mature to do so and appointed by his Father.

Growing in Christ to Think Like God

We must understand that, as growth has a natural process, so does the spiritual. However, it is no longer based on how much natural time passes in the Spirit that will cause us to grow and develop. Instead, it is dependent on how quickly we are to accept God's absolute truth and believe by faith that Jesus Christ paid the price for us to walk in abundant life. God is no respecter of a person's age, race, or anything. He requires nothing other than having faith in Him.

We see this in the life of Jesus Christ! After being born, He grew, and by the age of twelve, He was in the temple teaching and leaving those who were knowledgeable of God's Word in amazement. That is why I always encourage children, teens, adults, and elders to believe that God will do wonders with them because I know God's Word works for all who dare only to believe (see **Luke 2:46-52**).

Luke 2:52
"And Jesus increased in wisdom and stature, and favor with God and man."

Perhaps some might say, *"Yeah, but that was Jesus, the Son of God!"* Well, the Word of God teaches us that we are followers of Jesus. It also teaches us that the Word of God is for our development and benefit, so that we may be like Him. It is also proof that it is for anyone who believes in Him. Let us examine the Old Testament to find where it confirms that we, too, are to increase in wisdom and stature, growing in favor with God and with men.

I Samuel 3:19
"And Samuel grew, and the Lord was with him, and did let none of his words fall to the ground."

Here, we see how Samuel grew. In other words, he increased in wisdom and stature and favor with God and with men, so much so that all of Israel knew that he was to be a prophet of the Lord and that He was instructed by the Word of the Lord (see **I Samuel 3:20-21**). This example shows that it was not only Jesus, the Divine Son of God, who grew in wisdom and favor with God, but rather that Jesus operated as a man. However, he was the Son of God. Jesus Christ has been given to those of us who believe in Him as the supreme example of how to be sons of God on earth, who manifest in power and love for God's glory. Let us follow after the teaching of God's Word to mature as His offspring. To do this, we will have to know that God is not a liar and that what He says about us is true now and for all eternity (see **Hebrews 6:18**).

We must understand that for something to grow, it has its origin or starting point. For example, when someone is born out of the womb into this world, he or she is an infant or, in other words, a little baby. Any baby that is not cared for properly, though it has all the potential to become fully mature, will die if left to fend for itself. The same can be said about any born-again believers. Without good spiritual leaders who are full of the Holy Spirit to instruct them, they too will die spiritually speaking. They remain infants without developing into the fully manifested sons of God as born-again Christians, born in the Spirit of Christ Jesus. Allowing born-again believers to remain babies in the spirit must be avoided at all costs. Those who are more developed in the life of the Spirit of God must take up the mantle of helping develop babes in Christ to grow. By the guidance of the Spirit of God and His Word of faith rooted in love, to train them and send them out to fulfill the call God has for them in Jesus' name.

Notice that initially, a baby cannot talk or walk and needs to be cleaned and fed. That child is dependent on the care of a good parent or guardian to continue to live. A baby also pouts and is extremely needy almost every minute of the day, needing to be watched. A parallel spiritual truth exists for the born-again follower in Christ. The newborn in Christ demands constant care and attention.

Furthermore, they need to be taught how to talk and live by faith in God's Word by the Spirit. In my opinion, if a person is born again and is in an excellent bible-believing environment, it should not be more than three months to a year. Afterward, they can be assigned to serve and apply what they have learned. By this time, they should have learned just as a little child does how to walk, talk, play, and even begin to eat solid food, which will cause them to develop their thinking in the Spirit and even explore. All this is within the safety of the mature offspring (a mature believer). Leadership that the Lord has placed them under to ensure they are watched over and do not get hurt.

Afterward, they will grow into what we would call a young child or adolescent. At this point, they can think and process information and are taught to prepare their meals. They experience real hands-on work that develops into greater responsibilities that will make them secure and ready to work in the Kingdom of God. Here is the point where they are well-prepared to make the right decisions in obedience to God's Word. But, on the other hand, if they have a weak character that does not understand their new character in Christ, they tend to follow the crowd instead of leading it.

Decisions are what will cause a person to either succeed or fail in this life. As children of the Most-High God, we must aim to be all that Jesus Christ paid for us to be, which is to become full-grown children of God. To aspire to reach a mature status before the eyes of God, by His grace and favor. To rely solely upon God's instructions, which will lead us to provide for others. Work, talk, and think; lead and carry out orders that will allow God to bring His will here on earth as it is in Heaven.

God is waiting for the church through the Holy Spirit to develop each believer in Christ Jesus. To grow the believer to the point where they can be entrusted to govern, administer, and be sufficiently advanced to hear from God directly. Equally important is to receive His counsel to help guide and bring forth provision for others. Above all, to have a character that reflects the very character of God, thereby reaching that point where they can rule and reign in this life through the only one, Jesus Christ.

The question you should ask yourself with the Holy Spirit of God as your guide and teacher is: Where are you? Are you an unbeliever who does not know God? Are you unaware that all God wants for you is to be good and be the best? Or are you a believer who remains a baby in Christ, who cannot talk or understand things about the Kingdom of God in you? Do you know how to walk by faith in God's love to demonstrate your faith in an unbelieving world by the Holy Spirit? Do you know the Holy Spirit, a divine person and power who is God made available to you as a member of Christ?

As I am led to observe the state of the churches and congregations, I often find babies in Christ. These infants in Christ are of a carnal mindset and lustful expressions that have lasted many years and, sadly, even decades. Some are even under the false assumption that they are mature because they assume the Holy Spirit's gifts are in operation. However, the gifts of the Spirit are available to all who will believe. For instance, take a look at the church of Corinth. Their people were carnal and yet operated in the gifts that were given to them by the Holy Spirit (see **I Corinthians 3:1-4**).

It is time to make a sound decision. Declare this day to be the day you identify your starting point. It is the day you focus and choose to grow up to be all that God has made available for you. It is the day you let go of focusing on the things of this earth and begin to look only to Jesus Christ.

This dynamic change will only happen in your life as you choose daily to mortify the deeds of the flesh, which are sinful, and instead, you walk in the Spirit of God (see **Romans 8:11-19**). The word *mortifies* means to kill, become dead, and put to death. Please note that it is not talking about killing yourself. Instead, it is talking about killing the desires that will cause you and others pain. It is talking about killing every sinful act that your flesh, being inspired by evil, would try to have you commit. Paul, the apostle, said in **I Corinthians 15:31**, *"I die daily."*

The Doctrines of Christ

It is of utmost importance that we incorporate the foundation of the doctrines of Christ to be able to accomplish this life in the Spirit. We cannot move forward in edifying the things of the Lord unless the foundation is laid. He is the one who gives us the grace to be wise master builders (see **I Corinthians 3:10**).

The basic fundamental doctrines of Christ can be found in **Hebrews 6:1-2**. It will identify the doctrines of repentance from dead works; Faith toward God, the plurality of baptism, which includes submersion, as well as the Holy Ghost and fire, with the manifestation of the gifts of the Spirit as He wills. Be assured that the Holy Ghost's will is to empower every follower of Christ: only believe in the doctrine of laying on hands, the resurrection of the dead, and eternal judgment. These foundational truths are all necessary and must not be ignored. Allow the Holy Spirit to teach you these doctrines if you do not know them by searching them in the Bible.

Once we get the foundation right, we can be quickened to mortify the deeds of the flesh by the Spirit of God. Also, cast out the vain, imaginary thoughts that lead many to continue in a carnal mindset that leads them to lascivious conduct. God spoke to me by His Spirit saying, *"My people perish and are frustrated because they do not put My knowledge and My Word in action first in their lives. Therefore, they suffer and are destroyed as it is written in Hosea 4:6."* That very same verse explains that God rejects those that reject His knowledge, not because He rejects anyone, but instead because they reap instant death in their circumstances and situations from the decision to reject His counsel. God affirms us continually by the Holy Spirit's inspiration through **Romans 8:29-39;** God is merely telling us, *"I am for you, not against you. I made you My children, just like My Son Jesus. I give you all things and assure you nothing can separate you from My love for you."* However, instead of believing in God and His Word as the absolute truth. Many do not believe and are rejecting God's knowledge and, therefore, suffer just like the nonbeliever suffers. God has done everything to prove that we are His first love. Even so, no matter how much a person proves something to the one they are in a relationship with, the other person must choose to believe that expressed love. It is a decision, and they can choose to accept the love and enjoy the fullness of that love, or they can choose to reject that love and miss out on the benefit of being loved by that person.

Too many people do not believe or receive the love that God has for them, which causes them not to trust in God's provision. These are the ones who choose to continue putting their trust in the world's systems, like the days of Pharaoh, the king of Egypt, when Israel-the-Hebrews were their slaves. They are kept under a heavy burden and hard labor, all to eat crumbs. They work hard with much toil and sweat to barely get by. Then, having bought into the lie that Satan, the enemy of God and humanity, has placed in them, they settle and are thankful for the scraps.

This system of bondage is a great deception of the Enemy, who set up this world system and placed strongholds, thought patterns, and boundaries in the lives of those who have yet to be set free by the power of the Gospel of Jesus Christ. Satan keeps people under a slave and servant mentality, even though they have been set free through the perfect work of Jesus Christ on the Cross and his resurrection.

God, through Jesus Christ, has restored us into His image and likeness. He gave us the mentality of a king who would serve out of love in obedience to Him. He did not place us on earth to survive; He placed us on earth to work for His good pleasure and to create as He did. **Meditate on this: God worked and was delighted in His good work.** In other words, God took pleasure in His work and saw that it was good. So now we, who are made in His image and likeness, should work to create, as He did, for His glory, not just to get by and survive. Remember, God calls you his child, having embraced the loving sacrifice of Jesus Christ, by which your sins are forgiven. God continues to extend his gift of salvation to all people on the earth through Jesus Christ.

When God created the heavens and the earth and the entire host, He created the trees, plants, animals, the sun and moon, stars, galaxies, and even man. He did not do it for survival. God did it because it is His nature to create; God did it for pleasure. God said that He saw it and said it was good. Please note that it was good because God said it was so. Now, He gives us the ability to hear from Him, create, and call it good by His authority. Praise God for this privilege!

God has declared unto us to be imitators of Him (see **Ephesians 5:1**). So we are to operate just like Him. We should work and, at the end of each day, see progress and declare it is good. We should not complain and speak as some do, but instead, we should speak just like God.

Notice God ended His work because He finished. Nobody can end your work for you—it is your purpose, not theirs.

Human efforts could not terminate God-given assignments unless they were temporary assignments that require one to move on after a season of development. God does place us in different places for a season to learn something, but then God moves us. No matter what jobs you choose to take or not, never work for a living. Instead, live and work toward your purpose in life so that you, too, can rest and not grow frustrated. Like God, in whose image and likeness we are made, we are to create from within and then speak. As you speak it, it begins to be created so that you, too, can look at the end of each day and say, **"It was good."**

If you observe in Genesis chapter one, God creates everything within Himself and has everything finished in the invisible realm. In Genesis chapter two, God manifests what comes from the invisible realm to the visible realm. The amazing thing is that He is continuing to manifest Himself right now, even at this very moment, as I am writing this book and you are reading it. He created this, and it is being carried out just as He designed it to be, but it is already done. The inspiration of God was upon man to name all creatures. God put a man to rule, subdue the earth, and make it like the Kingdom of Heaven, for this visible earth is a part of His Kingdom. God indwells in us, His believers. He who indwells in us designed us initially only to receive His loving instructions. To bring about the best on earth as it is in Heaven (see **I John 4:4 and Genesis 1:26-30**).

I simply cannot emphasize enough the importance of looking unto Jesus Christ as our only example of who we are as sons of God. Jesus said in **John 14:12b,** *"Greater works will you do in my name!"* **(John 6:28-29)**—Our ability to do the greater works relies solely on our ability to believe that Jesus Christ is the Son of God. Jesus reestablished us to our original state of being before sin ever came into the picture. We must believe in His love and integrity. God is genuinely more trustworthy than anyone you have ever trusted. We must walk fearlessly to bring about the manifestation and proof of the Kingdom of God by the Holy Spirit, who is our Helper and Teacher, giving life to the written Word of God.

In **I John 3:1-3 and 4:16-21**, God has declared that we are His first love. He calls us sons, heirs with Christ Jesus, and though we only have partial knowledge in this world, the Word of God says that when He appears and we see Him, we will come to see that we are just like Him. He is pure; therefore, we are pure. While in this world, we continue to purify ourselves by believing in Him and His perfect work. God has favored us to have His very nature as born-again believers, and we must walk without worry and fear of anything that comes our way. We are to enforce the authority and power of Jesus that we have in us and bring anything out of line with the Kingdom of God on earth.

Faith in God's love through Jesus Christ is the key to eradicating all fear and intimidation of the enemy. The enemy has held people in bondage by deceiving many saints of God into believing that they are walking in humility by confessing things that sound spiritual. Things like, *"I am just a sinner saved by grace!"* Not anymore! The Word of God says in **I John 4:18** that we must know that His love is perfect and trustworthy above all. Our confidence, security, and assurance in His love toward us allow us to cast out all fear. All the enemy throws our way: debates, gossip, strife, neglect, depression, poverty, hate, envy, jealousy, sickness, death, and other evil things. As we do this, we operate in love with our brothers and sisters and meet all needs. The body of Christ should fill the earth with God's glory. Filling the world with God's glory is to be done through God's blessing. The first man lost the blessing because of sin; however, the blessing is restored to us through Jesus Christ.

God has set this up so that if we receive what He has made us, we can say, as Jesus said, *"The Father that dwelleth in me, he doeth the works,* (see **John 14:10**)." We can take all that Jesus provided for us by His death, burial, and resurrection, for He has credited it all to our account. Jesus has given His merits to us who believe because He does not need them for Himself. He is and always has been, from the beginning to the end, Righteous, Holy, and King above all.

The words we are to speak are to be the Father's Word, not our own. This is a wake-up call to come out of being babies and little children in the Kingdom of God and become mature, manifested sons and daughters of God in this earthly realm who hear, believe, and obey God's Word for His glory.

We are to be as the ram's horn in the right hand of God the Father. The sound of God's Living Word comes out of us, declaring to all humanity by the inspiration of the Holy Spirit, "It is Jubilee; **your sins are forgiven; your debt has been paid in full. You have been delivered, set free, and you can now partake of the fullness of the blessing of God that maketh rich, and he adds no sorrow with it.**"(see **Proverbs 10:22**) HalleluYah!

"Restoring Mankind's
True Identity"

CHAPTER THREE

*Being Disciplined and
Courageous
To-Do the Word
of God*

Being Disciplined and Courageous to Do the Word Of God

We must be disciplined and courageous to do the Word of God, just like Jesus. He grew, and so must we. He disciplined His body and lost sight of all selfishness, and so must we. He carried out only what He heard and saw God the Father do. Though Jesus had his soul as a man, He never operated from the lust of the flesh, giving a carnal opinion. Instead, Jesus only spoke what He heard the Father speak (see **John 14:10**).

Some people might not like the word discipline because they associate it with being mistreated. Perhaps while growing up, a parent, guardian, or even an authority figure at school or work misused the word, causing you to want to reject it. Let me assure you that the word "discipline" is a blessing when used correctly, as God always does.

For clarity and understanding, allow me to define the words discipline and courage to remove any wrong perceptions and ideas. The word *"discipline"* means: *instructing or educate; to inform the mind; to prepare by instructing in correct principles and habits; as to discipline youth for a profession or future usefulness* (Webster). The word *"courage"* means: *the quality of mind or spirit that enables a person to face difficulties, dangers, pain, circumstances, etc., without any fear; bravery* (Webster).

As mentioned earlier, Jesus Christ's original Hebrew name is Y'shua Messiah. Jesus is our only example of a full measure-manifested Son of God, which is what every believer has been made. Remember, God sowed His Son to reap many sons. "For whom he did foreknow, he also did predestinate to be conformed to the image of his Son, that he might be the firstborn among many brethren" (**Romans 8:29**).

Why was Jesus Christ, as a man, able to manifest the

Kingdom of God to the visible world? Jesus Christ was able to manifest the Kingdom of God to the visible world by complete discipline and focus on God's instruction and teaching. He did precisely as His Father in both works and words. Jesus was disciplined and obedient. By learning to love the discipline of God the Father. One can begin to see how loving God's discipline will lead us to prosperity and abundance. This discipline leads to His best for us in ways that cannot be obtained through any other source or effort. Jesus Christ was not worried about what people thought about Him or whether He was famous. The only thing on His heart, mind, and body was to do the will of the Father. He only cared about how our Heavenly Father looked at Him, and so must we.

Looking upon the life of Jesus Christ, we see that He had the mentality and follow-through for what God, the Father, instructed Him to do, despite how He looked to those around Him. He boldly carried out those instructions at all costs. In **Matthew 12:9-14**, Jesus restores the withered hand of a man and does not care what the religious Pharisees would say about Him or do to Him, for that matter. Unlike people today who are worried about their appearance for those around them. Believers in Christ, you must realize that those around you, those worrisome people, cannot help you. God has sent you in the midst of them to help them because He has restored His blessing on you to fix everything around you by indwelling in you.

Yes, you may look crazy to them at times, and even weird. However, it will not make any difference once God shows up and shines through you, simply because you chose to be disciplined and courageous to do the work of God. The results will lead you and me to become the expressed, visible image of the invisible God in this visible world. You and I are made the Living Word to those around us. Why? Jesus is in us, and greater is He who is in us than he who is in the world (see **I John 4:4**).

Mark 5:39-43 Speaks of a little damsel who died, **yet Jesus, being disciplined and courageous, says, "She is not dead; she is asleep."** They laughed at Him, and He threw them all out. Think about this: Jesus Christ kicked them out along with their unbelief and expectation of a funeral. The action that Jesus took at this funeral, to the **carnal-minded person** (who is a person that has no spiritual understanding of God and relies only on the information given through the visible world system and holds a natural perspective), is interpreted by the carnal-minded person as rude. Nevertheless, be assured that if you do as Jesus did, who was rooted in love and walked by faith to solve problems or help others. God's will is manifested, and the results will glorify God, not fallen humanity.

More than once, I have told a believer who should know better. To be quiet, even when people have hurt them, and the beginning symptoms of bitterness are coming about, or when the beginning of depression comes about because someone passes from this life to the next, the **natural man** says, **"Poor you,"** **what are you going to do?** The **born-again** believer responds just like Jesus, being disciplined and courageous. **The believer begins to give them the Word of life that leads them out of depression and ushers them into celebrating eternal life in Christ Jesus.** Jesus is calling us to be just like Him. Jesus calls us to total freedom from this world and those who are not abiding in the light. He is calling us His children to bring the dead to life and to give us all to eat of his goodness (see **Romans 4:17**).

In **John 11:38-44**, we see Jesus at Lazarus' tomb declaring to his sister Martha that 'he,' referring to Lazarus, will rise again. Many must have said this guy, Jesus, is crazy; Lazarus has been dead for four days and even stinks now. Again, He demonstrates God's power. Jesus shows His plan here on how He would use those who followed Him to bring the dead to life by the obedience of the Living Word, removing the stone, and calling forth the dead to come alive. Glory to God!

Jesus Christ had received instruction on the things of the Kingdom of God. He had the quality of mind and follow-through that, for anything God the Father instructed Him to do, He did it, and He did it fearlessly. What led Jesus (Y'shua) to be this way? He was totally in sync with God, our Heavenly Father, despite the many opportunities on this earth to be distracted. He made it easy for us by taking what He did and applying it to our account so that we can now function as He does. He made His righteousness to be ours, along with His power, grace, and love. Everything Jesus did was not for him but rather for you and me to be able to operate like Him. All He is and has; He has now made us to be and also have.

God Cannot Lie

Here is the big question? If this is the truth, and it is. **Then what is keeping it from manifesting itself in people's lives?** Before answering this, let us read three scriptures. First, **Romans 3:4a**, *"Let God be true and every man a liar."* Second, **Titus 1:2a**, *"which God, that cannot lie."* Third, **Hebrews 6:18** says, *"That by two immutable things, in which **it was impossible for God to lie**, we might have a strong consolation, who have fled for refuge to lay hold upon the hope set before us:"*

The answer to this question is that many people still have not believed the Word of God that says **God is not a liar, and God cannot lie.** Some people find it easier to believe someone who has lied to them often rather than God. God has never lied to them and has a proven record of always keeping His word to those who believe in Him. **Many have not come to trust and solely rely on God and His love for us**. In **First John 4:16-18**, John confessed that he and those with him had known and believed God's love for them. They believed that they knew God, who is Love, and they operated fearlessly and free from torment.

I do not want to offend anyone, so please hear me. Although God has declared, *"Fight the good fight of FAITH, you have professed a good profession before many witnesses"* (see **I Timothy 6:12**). God also declared, *"Be strong and of good courage (be daring and fearless of anything that comes your way), for I will not fail you, and I am with you wherever you go"* (see **Joshua 1:5-9**). Although God encouraged us with these words, many are fearful, and many are weak in faith. The answer I have given is the truth, and I give it to you because I love God and His people. It is not God's best for His children to be crying, begging, complaining, and fearful because He has given everything to us already. He is a good God, and He will never fail us.

Learn to receive His discipline and instructions fearlessly, doing what He says regardless of what the outward, temporary circumstances are telling you. If anyone is fearful, it is because they do not know God's love or trust Him. I have GOOD NEWS. Today is your day! He wants to have communion with you if you make that decision right now. Develop your trust in God, and you will no longer be defeated in life.

God made it simple for all to have access to His best. To receive His best, He made the **COMMON DENOMINATOR OF FAITH ROOTED IN LOVE** to be the motive for **anyone** who would believe, but you must **BELIEVE ON HIM**. Perhaps right now, you stand convicted of not fully trusting in God. Notice, I said convicted, not condemned. Do not worry—God is bringing you out right now as you shift to believe Him and solely live by His Word. God has a proven track record. He delivered you before, and He will not fail you now.

God does not bring His Word to condemn but rather to heal and make you whole. So what must we do? We must renew our minds! *"Be not conformed to this world: but be ye transformed by the renewing of your mind, that ye may prove what is that good, and acceptable, and perfect, will of God"* (**Romans 12:2**). In the coming chapters, we will go more in-depth on how to renew the mind.

We must stop looking at the mirror of the flesh, which is a lying mirror, and look at the mirror of the Word of God that shows us exactly who we are and how God sees us through Jesus Christ (see **James 1:22-26**). A more in-depth study and revelation of the mirror of Truth can be found in my book *"What Do You See in the Mirror? Mirror, Mirror, Flesh or Spirit?"* But for now, meditate on the fact that Jesus Christ shows exactly who God has made you by His grace.

Are you still thinking it is impossible, hopeless, or not working, and that you are not good enough? Then, you will have to rebuke that lying spirit and pull down the stronghold Satan has in your soul, in Jesus' name. If you are of God, you are no longer under the limitations of the natural realm nor the powers of darkness as before, when you were not saved. You are now as Jesus is in Heaven. Remember, according to **1 John 4:17-18**, that your right standing with God is that of Jesus Christ's right standing with God the Father. Now, you are to rule and reign in this life rooted in God's love by one Jesus Christ (see **Romans 5:17**).

All of God's creation is waiting for you to help it, those who are not saved through Jesus Christ. Again, I ask that you meditate on the facts of what **1 John 4:17-18** teaches us. Jesus is King of kings, ONE with the Father, and has all authority in Heaven and Earth. Jesus has all wisdom, power, and riches. Jesus is Lord over all kingdoms. Now, I want you to look at yourself in the mirror and say, **"As Jesus is in Heaven, so am I now in this world."** HalleluYah!

Furthermore, take a look at two verses of scripture in the **third chapter of Galatians**. **Verse 16** states, *"Now to*

Abraham and his seed were the promises made. He saith not, and to seeds, as of many; but as of one, And to thy seed, which is Christ." **Verse 29** states, *"And if ye be Christ's, then are ye Abraham's seed, and heirs according to the promise."* Every born-again believer is of Christ; therefore, we are Abraham's seed and heirs.

Indeed, what an honor God has given us. The Word of God also says:

> And if children, then heirs; heirs of God, and joint-heirs with Christ; if so be that we suffer with him, that we may be also glorified together. For I reckon that the sufferings of this present time are not worthy to be compared with the glory, which shall be revealed in us. **(Romans 8:17-18)**

I want you to see that you and I are joint heirs with Christ, meaning that what He has, we have, and so does anyone else who is a born-again believer. As we have received this inheritance, it does come with suffering. This suffering is not the same type of suffering defined by the world and those who are carnally-minded. The word **suffering** means hardships, but notice, no matter what problems came toward Jesus, our example, He overcame them, and with Him, so do we in His name.

Furthermore, look at how Jesus never suffered sickness. He never suffered deficiencies, and He never suffered in the sense that people often consider suffering. The life of Jesus on this earth did not include defeat or giving up. Jesus did not suffer a lack of provision in the natural or in the spirit. If He needed something, it was there instantly for Him. He was not depressed, feeling lonely, complaining, and pouting. No! He was full of joy and compassion. However, the type of suffering he endured was from the disbelief of others. He knew the original way the **first Man** was created to rule the earth and saw how humanity was living so beneath the quality of life

God had provided. He also suffered from how Satan had deceived and blinded so many. However, on the Cross, Jesus overcame all by willingly laying down His life for all the sins of humanity so that they could live as they believed in Him.

Yes, Jesus suffered for a moment, but not in comparison to eternity in the fullness of His total and complete victory. Jesus suffered the ignorance of others. He suffered the hurt of others. The things that Jesus did then, we as the Body of Christ, should be doing now. As many as have come to Him, Jesus Christ made them whole.

People are hurting in this world, and you are the one whom God placed in the midst of them. You and I are believers in God. We are members of the body of Christ, who are equipped by Him, as we receive His instructions and obey them as His courageous soldiers. As sons of God, He has commissioned us to go to the entire world and make them whole in Jesus' name.

We are to heal the sick, deliver the captives, raise the dead, and help as many as come to us. For we abide in Christ, and we are a conduit in this earth for Him to operate through. He longs by His Spirit to make those around us whole. Nevertheless, frequently, we do not let God touch the people around us. The reason? Our inconsistency in remaining strong in faith, rooted in love, and believing that God is not a liar.

Remember, actions speak louder than words! We are God's legal access to this earthly realm. In order for us to follow God's directions and execute His instructions. We must first go to the Word of God, then think upon it, meditate on it, speak it, and act upon it— doing all that the Word of God tells us to do. What we think, speak, and meditate on matters. **Proverbs 23:7** tells us, "*As you think of yourself in your heart, so are you.*" This is a principle. We must think of ourselves in our hearts the way God thinks of us, and then use our spoken words. The Words you choose to speak will navigate you in the direction of your most influential thoughts; **James 3:2-18** speaks of this matter. Use your steering wheel, which is your tongue, to lead you to sow into the Spirit so that you can reap life. **Proverbs 18:21** informs us that "***Death and life are in the power of the tongue: and they that love it shall eat the fruit thereof.***" Do not use your tongue to reap death.

Make sure the treasures in your heart are good treasures of the Word of God. Otherwise, you will continue to suffer defeat, which is not what God has for you. It is easy to know if you have good fruit. All you have to do is listen to yourself talk! **Luke 6:45** applies to this truth. What you speak is what is in your mind. If you know that what you have been speaking is not of God, then remove the evil things from your mind. Discipline yourself to receive the instruction and education of the Kingdom of God, in the Word of God, and begin to choose life today.

Saints of God, I believe God wants us to prosper now more than ever. Therefore, when others are worried due to pandemics, wars, abuse of authority, and divisions, we are fearlessly courageous and taking ground, ever-increasing in faith, love, and wealth, spiritually and materially. Having good, Godly success will bear witness to all that Jesus is Lord. We will not just keep the blessings God has given us, but become a blessing to all the families of the earth. Partaking and fulfilling the Word of God in Christ as Abraham's seed— "*in thee shall all families of the earth be blessed*" (see **Genesis 12:3**). For the believers, the Saints of God, to become doers of the Word, it will take discipline and courage, for there is no other way. We must follow our Lord and do what He did and even greater things in His name, for He is working with us to do it (see **John 14:12**).

There is no magic pill. We must go to the Word of God, read it, meditate on it, speak it, and do it daily and consistently. Jesus Christ did it in this manner, and this is the way we must do it! Be completely focused on the Father's instructions, which He left written in the bible, the Word of God. Be courageous enough to do it without worrying about our reputation in the eyes of others.

God has placed it in my heart to remind you to stop worrying about your needs. He has provided everything you need and even what you want if you just believe Him. Consider my children; they eat for free and do not pay rent or a mortgage. They enjoy paid vacations, and transportation is free for them. They live debt-free, and not only do they have their needs met, but they also get what they want. How much more is our Heavenly Father, who knows we need all these things and desires to give us His best? Do you think you are a better father or parent than God? All you have to do is ask God for His good gifts, believe in Him, and do what His word says to do to have it.

That is what He has done for me, and He is willing to do for you, no matter your circumstances. **Matthew 7:11** reads, *"If ye then, being evil, know how to give good gifts unto your children, how much more shall your Father which is in heaven give good things to them that ask him?"* The Word of God also says, *"If ye then, being evil, know how to give good gifts unto your children: how much more shall your heavenly Father give the Holy Spirit to them that ask him?"* (**Luke 11:13**). God has done this for my home, and if you believe Him, He will do it for yours too.

"Restoring Mankind's True Identity"

CHAPTER FOUR

Restoring the Mind and Mindset of Christ as your own

Restoring the Mind And Mindset Of Christ As Your Own

As believers in Christ, the Holy Spirit speaks to our <u>spirit</u> as they are one (**1 Corinthians 6:17**). Then our spirit communicates to our sound <u>mind</u> **(2 Timothy 1:7)** through the imagination that introduces the ability to think on God's thoughts and instructions through His Spoken Word. Finally, we use our <u>will</u> to decide what to manifest on the earth. If we have faith and obey God, our decision will be to His glory. However, if we choose not to believe God's Word, we will get the same outcome as the world in sin.

The scriptural support in this chapter is referenced from:

> **I Corinthians 2:16**
> For **who hath known the mind of the Lord**, that he may instruct him? but **we have the mind of Christ**.

> **Philippians 2:5 -7**
> Let **this mind be in you, which was also in Christ Jesus**: 6 Who, **being in the form of God, thought it not robbery to be equal with God**: 7 But made himself of no reputation, and took upon him the form of a servant, and was made in the likeness of men:

> **Philippians 3:15**
> Let us therefore, as many as **be perfect, be thus minded**: and if in anything ye be otherwise minded, **God shall reveal even this unto you.** (Completely dead to the things of the world and living by Christ and He alone!)

> **Ephesians 4:23**
> And be **renewed in the spirit of your mind**;

Romans 12:2
And be not conformed to this world: but be ye transformed by the **renewing** of your **mind**, that ye may prove what is that good, and acceptable, and perfect, will of God.

In order to embrace the Mind and Mindset of Christ, we will get the definitions of these words to gain a clear understanding.

Mind—that which is responsible for one's thoughts and feelings.

To Mind—*to attend to or regard with submission to obey* (Webster), the power that conceives, judges or reasons. It has to do with your thoughts and what they are inclined toward. To fix thoughts on, to regard with attention, your deep thoughts, intentions, desires and understanding, purpose, and design.

Mindset—the ideas and attitudes in which a person approaches a situation. It is the habits of mind formed by previous experiences or situations. In this, you must now renounce your old mindset and embrace **the mindset of Christ.** This change is necessary because: (1) before Christ Jesus, you were right to fear the enemy; (2) before Christ Jesus, you were right to know it was beyond your ability; (3) before Christ, when a problem arose, you were right to worry and doubt.

These things were so because you were ignorant of what Christ Jesus had already done for you, in that you were still under the kingdom of darkness. But now, if you are a believer in Christ, you have no right to fear, doubt, or say something is impossible. You have no right to contradict the Word of God or what He has done for you. Do you know why? It is because He has declared unto us, who believe in Him, that He will never leave nor fail us. He will never allow anything to harm us, and we must do what He says, which is **ONLY BELIEVE!** You can confirm this by reading **John 6:28-29 and Joshua 1:5.**

Now, although this is work, it is work without toil if we know how to trust only in God (see **Proverbs 3:5-6**). I often ask myself, why would anyone want to be defeated if they can walk in victory? The obvious answer is that if everyone knew they did not have to put their head down in shame because they failed, but instead, through Christ, they can now hear from God. As they obey Him, the result will be no defeats, and this would cause people to run to God and not from Him. Believers struggling with frustration must renounce mindsets and behaviors learned in the world. Then, embrace the mindset and actions of who they abide in, Christ Jesus.

I need you to confidently know that God's Word is true to understand what God has already given you. We just read in **I Corinthians 2:16** that we know the mind of the Lord because He gave it to us. He has made us one with it as the word abides in us. The apostle Paul said in **Romans 1:15,** "*As much as in me is I am ready to preach the gospel.*" How did it get in him? God put it there as he meditated on the scriptures: it became alive and one with him.

Without a doubt, who knows the mind of the Lord? We do praise God! Who can instruct Him? We can if we truly abide in the Spirit and not the lust of the flesh. How is this possible? It is possible because it is God in us, for we no longer live, but Christ lives in us. We are the ones in whom He has revealed His Word by His Spirit. HalleluYah—now do you believe or not?

I remember once in prayer that God spoke to me by the Holy Spirit and said, "*If I were to show you in My Word, My Truth, and it did not agree with what you have believed all this time, would you let go of your own opinion or what others opinion is of Me and take Me for Who I tell you I am and all I* have done for you?" I said, "Yes, I would, Lord." He then said, "*Many are quick to say yes, but when they are faced with My Truth as I declare in My Word, of Myself, and it challenges them to let go of what they have believed, they soon find themselves in a fight, in their soul. Only those that truly trust Me can let go of themselves and watch Me show up and show out all that I have declared to them, regardless of how impossible it seems.*" I believe God is speaking to you right now, asking you the same question. Listen, my brother and sister, if you take His Word above all else, you will see His Glory.

I am here to declare to you that if you listen and obey the instructions of God's Word, defeat will have no place in your life. Now, this takes discipline, determination, focus, time, and everything you are. It takes all of you, your spirit, soul, and body, to focus on the reality that the old you was put to death. The power of God's Spirit in you now allows you to have the victory and embrace the new creature, the son of God, that He made you in Christ Jesus, remember the old man is dead (see **Colossians 3:3**). This new position causes you to rule and reign as a king in life under the authority of the King of kings who is, Jesus Christ (see **Romans 5:17**). This new reality in Spirit and Truth is exciting. Brothers and sisters, we are now going to look at the attitude of how Jesus approached the different things He faced while here on earth. We will see His habitual responses and mental disposition. We will see how He responds to situations and expects us to do the same as followers of Him.

The **mindset of Christ is bold**, and so is yours if you are in Christ Jesus. He **cast out all devils** when those around Him were either possessed or oppressed by them (see **Acts 10:38 and Matthew 8:16**). He **healed the sick (Mark 1:34 and Matthew 14:14)** and **forcefully opposed injustice (Mark 11:15)**. He had **zero tolerance for unbelief** to the point that he kicked everyone out at a funeral and only allowed those who believed to stay with Him. Here, Jesus was teaching us to cast out all unbelief and not conform to the way things appear in the natural order of things, even when something seems to be dead (see **Luke 8:54**).

Jesus feared nothing (see **Luke 8:50**). Fear NOT is what He continually said and taught (see **Luke 12:32**). He loved all and defended the weak (see **Luke 17:2** and **Matthew 18:10**). He reproved the self-righteous (**John 8:42-58**) and had an abundance mentality that is not lacking, no matter what He saw in the natural world (see **Mark 6:35-42** and **John 6:4-12**). Jesus Christ gives life to the dead even when they stink, and all hope is lost as He did with the daughter of Jairus, and also with Lazarus (see **Luke 8:54-56** about Jairus' daughter, **and John 11:14-44** about Lazarus). He educated people—teaching about the kingdom and what was available to all who believed in Him and modeled the type of life every believer is to demonstrate (see **Matthew 9:35** and **Acts 1:1**). He corrected false teachings in **Matthew 23:13-30** and desired for all to be empowered to empower others (see **Matthew 28:19** and **Mark 16**).

The mindset of Christ is a mountain-moving one. It is a mindset that can bless those who choose to believe God and curse the unfruitful works of the enemy (see **Mark 11:20-24**). The mindset of Christ is one that binds and loosens from the unseen realm to the seen realm. It takes the provision and authority of the Kingdom of God to destroy the operations of the evil one (see **Matthew 18:18-19**). The mindset of Christ sets the captive free and shows mercy and grace (see **Luke 4:18; Mark 10:46-52** and **John 1:17**).

The mindset of Christ forgives (see **Matthew 6:15; 9:5-7**, and **Ephesians 1:7**) and is one of dominion and ruler-ship (see **Revelations 17:14; 19:16**). It speaks those things that be not as though they were, in that the mindset of Christ is the mindset of God. It is also a mindset of resurrection power (see **John 11:25**), and anything you speak to in the Spirit from the mindset of Christ will not remain dead. Therefore, in Jesus' name, speak, bless, decree, and live (see **Romans**

4:17). Are you glad? Are you rejoicing that you have the mindset of Christ to approach everything in the light of this revelation? Know that it is only by Jesus Christ our Lord—for it is He in us, the hope of Glory (see **Colossians 1:27**). HalleluYah.

You Have a Choice to Make

This hope of glory in us, mentioned in Colossians 1:27, is good news. It is by Grace that we are saved because of Christ Jesus. We have been made the righteousness of God through Him and in Him. Therefore, you and I are now the righteousness of God in Him, and we have the mind of Christ. However, it is a choice to walk in the Spirit and believe His Word, be one with His mind in us, or choose to continue in the flesh and the ways that the enemy has taught us through this world system. Even those who have confessed Jesus as their Lord. If they continue to live by the methods of the world, they will continue to get the same results as the world, which leaves them empty and void of life and with no joy. We must choose now to consciously act upon the Word of God by the Spirit every second of this life to operate as God designed.

To get one hundred percent results, we must speak the words of Father God. He speaks to us through the Holy Spirit through the Word of God in Christ Jesus, in whom we now abide. We are one as members of the Body of Christ and must be obedient in only speaking what He tells us to speak.

John 8:26 *"I have many things to say and to judge of you: but he that sent me is true; and **I speak to the world those things which I have heard of him.**"*

Saints of God, we should not be speaking what we want selfishly, nor as the world has taught us. Speaking out of the selfish mind is over if we truly want God's best for all people. We will have to deny the lustful mindset and only speak what we hear from God through His Spirit.

> Then said Jesus unto them, When ye have lifted up the Son of man, then shall ye know that I am he, and that **I do nothing of myself; but as my Father hath taught me, I speak these things. And he that sent me is with me: the Father hath not left me alone; for I do always those things that please him**. (John 8:28-29)

This Grace is given to us, and this new covenant ensures that God reminds our minds that we have the mind of Christ because He put it there.

> For this is the covenant that I will make with the house of Israel after those days, saith the Lord; **I will put my laws into their mind, and write them in their hearts:** and I will be to them a God, and they shall be to me a people: (**Hebrews 8:10**)

> This is the covenant that I will make with them after those days, saith the Lord, **I will put my laws into their hearts, and in their minds** will I write them; (**Hebrews 10:16**)

One of the problems that exists for many believers today is conforming to the ways of this world. Settling to be saved by Grace but remaining with an intellectual, reasoning mind of self-effort instead of possessing the supernatural mind of Christ by faith. There are many examples of carnal believers in the body of Christ in the Bible who were living far beneath their son-ship rights as sons of God—do not let that be you. Do not settle for being in the same boat as those who are still under bondage and the curse of the law of sin and death, especially when Christ has redeemed us from the curse (see **Galatians 3:13**).

You have been set free, but it is up to you to believe and

take on Christ's mindset. Christ's mindset says you will not fear, and you will not be in doubt. You will not be defeated: you are a giant slayer, you are a dispeller of darkness, you are from above and not beneath you speak and create because your words are the words of the Living God that will never return to Him void. You are the oracles of God, ministering with the fullness of His ability.

> If any man speak, let him **speak as the oracles of God;** if any man minister, let him do it as of the ability which God giveth: that God in all things may be glorified through Jesus Christ, to whom be praise and dominion for ever and ever. Amen. (**1Peter 4:11**)

God has spoken you; He will perform you as you yield (see **Jeremiah 1:12**).

The mindset of Christ is the mindset of God; therefore, according to **Jeremiah 1:7-10**, this is as one that has the mindset of God—you root out, pull down, destroy, throw down all that is not the knowledge of the mindset of Christ, and you build and plant with all that is His Word.

Proverbs 28:1 *"The wicked flee when no man pursueth: but the righteous are bold as a lion."*

You and I are of the **mindset** that knows it is the righteousness of God. Therefore, we are **bold as a lion** and are **dominating** and **roaring God's Word** to send all devils trembling in the name of Jesus, the Messiah. To do this, we must comprehend and understand by faith in God's wisdom that our intellect was limited in the old nature before we gave our lives to Christ. But now, in the new nature, which is spirit —supernatural, we are enabled to have a supernatural understanding if we take it by faith.

Understanding means *to be able to comprehend knowledge, exact comprehension; intelligence; agreement of* *minds; union of sentiments.* When you **understand**, you are empowered to become one with the person instructing you in their understanding. Of course, you can choose to reject the understanding. Therefore, you will not be able to see how the one giving the instruction is operating because you willfully reject knowledge. The scripture declares in **Amos 3:3**, *"Can two walk together, except they be agreed?"* It is time to agree with the Word and be one with the Word. It is time to know that as the Body of Christ, we are the Living Word in action that responds to every situation and circumstance as Christ Jesus responds to it in Heaven. We must remember that **as He is in Heaven, so are we in this world** (see **I John 4:17-18**).

It is time to let go of our own opinions and thoughts, along with our reasoning, and embrace God's thoughts and His knowledge. We must move from self-opinion and embrace knowing and enforcing the absolute truth that is His Word. We must realize the Word of God is His mind and attitude left for us to know. The Word leads us to become one with Him on earth, being led by the Holy Spirit. As the Church, we are His conduit to bring His goodness to all His creation. Now, if believers choose not to yield to the Holy Spirit, their defeat in this life will continually manifest itself. Still, suppose they ever arise to faith in God's Word with action being without regard to self-opinion or self-reasoning. In that case, their victory in this life will always manifest itself. God is true. Every man and circumstance that would dare try to arise against His knowledge will be arrested and brought into the obedience of Christ. The manifestation of God's best will manifest continually from victory to victory through the good fight of faith (see **Romans 3:4**). It is time to live twenty-four hours a day, seven days a week, fighting the good fight of faith, which is the only fight we, as believers, are called to (see **I Timothy 6:12**).

The mindset of Christ honors God and loves God by putting to mind all that God has said to do. Therefore, as we obey Him and accept what He says to do without doubting His instructions, this mindset allows God's command to be the visible expression manifested on this earth through us, born-again believers.

Matthew 22:37
*"Jesus said unto him, Thou shalt love the Lord thy God with all thy heart, and with all thy soul, and **with all thy mind**."*

Mark 12:30
*"And thou shalt love the Lord thy God with all thy heart, and with all thy soul, and **with all thy mind**, and with all thy strength: this is the first commandment."*

Luke 10:27
*"And he answering said, Thou shalt love the Lord thy God with all thy heart, and **with all thy soul**, and with all thy strength, **and with all thy mind**; and thy neighbour as thyself."*

Do as Mary did, **cast into your mind all that the Word of God is saying** and declare as Mary declared, *"**be it unto me according to thy word**."* (see **Luke 1:38**)

Luke 1:29
*"And when she saw him, **she was troubled at his saying, and cast in her mind** what manner of salutation this should be."*

Like Mary, the Believer is Mother to Jesus

For some, the mother of Jesus, known as Mary, is believed to be born without sin due to their religious doctrine. However, most people do not know that even the early Church fathers in the Roman Catholic Church did not have this belief, and that this doctrine goes against the scriptures of what the Bible teaches concerning Mary. **Like Mary, believers in Christ are now the mother of Jesus, the womb and channel through which the Living Word of God comes into manifestation from the unseen realm to the seen realm.** I will be expanding on this to know how God desires us to give birth to Jesus Christ. Bear with me and allow me to explain what God has revealed to me by the Holy Spirit in line with the Word of God.

The definition of the word **MOTHER** in the STRONG Concordance #517 in HEBREW means *"Union of Family."* (*The mother is the wife and gives birth to children.*)

The word <u>Mother</u> means: Womb, Matrix, the Channel of a river, that which has produced anything (Noah Webster, 1828).

The word <u>Matrix</u> means:

> The womb, the cavity in which the fetus of an animal is formed and nourished till birth; a mold; the cavity in which anything is formed, and which gives it shape; as the matrix of a type; the place in where anything is formed or produced. (Noah Webster, 1828)

The word <u>Womb</u> means: *the place where anything is produced* (Noah Webster, 1828).

In summary, the definition of **Mother** is the Channel of the river that produces something; the Womb, where the seed is nurtured and grows until it is born—the place where something is formed or produced.

In the Gospel of **John Chapter 2, verses 1 through 12**, we will discover how a believer in God's Word becomes a mother to Jesus. We will see what qualifies you to be a mother to Jesus, the mother's motive, and what actions must be taken to birth the divine child God has placed in you as you receive His Word. We will then see how, once He is born, we are to serve Him to as many as will drink this wonderful new wine. We shall also see that God has made those who become mothers to Jesus dispensers of this new wine, causing all who indeed drink of it never to want anything else.

John 2:1
"And the third day there was a marriage in Cana of Galilee; and the mother of Jesus was there:"

The **third day**, or the number 3, signifies divinity, a perfect testimony, and complete and perfect unity. In **I John 5:6-7**, *"For there are three that bear record in heaven, the Father, the Word, and the Holy Ghost; and these three are one."* In **Matthew 28:19**, *"Go ye therefore, and teach all nations, baptizing them in the name of the Father, and of the Son, and of the Holy Ghost."* Of Testimony, **Deuteronomy 17:6** says, *"At the mouth of two witnesses or three witnesses, shall he that is worthy of death be put to death."* **Matthew 12:40** tells us that in **three days and three nights**, the Son of man was in the heart of the earth, a complete number. Furthermore, **Deuteronomy 19:15** states, *"One witness shall not rise up against a man for any iniquity, or for any sin, in any sin that he sinneth: at the mouth of two witnesses, or at the mouth of three witnesses, shall the matter be established."*

Interestingly enough, in **Ezekiel 14:14-20**, God declares

that even if **Noah, Daniel, and Job** were in a land that He is judging because the people of the land have strayed away from Him, only Noah, Daniel, and Job would be delivered by their righteousness. **Notice the three people lived in different times when they walked the earth, yet they are mentioned as a perfect testimony.** Why? As I asked God this question, the Holy Spirit revealed to me that the meaning of their names was the revelation of this prophetic declaration.

Noah means *Rest*; **Daniel** means *Judge from God, composed of two words, one that means all-powerful*, and **Job** means *hated and persecuted* (Strong Concordance). **By the Spirit of God's revelation, we see that He who gives rest and is Judge from God was hated and persecuted. So that only the one who abides in Him, Him being Yeshua-Jesus, can be saved and delivered.**

Exodus 23:14 gives a perfect testimony of three feasts, a Divine time of celebration. In **Exodus 23:17**, man is to be presented before the Lord perfectly and completely through the perfect testimony. **Ecclesiastes 4:12** speaks of *a threefold cord, which cannot be quickly broken*. All of this establishes that **in the number 3, there is perfect unity and testimony.** So the scripture in **John 2:1**, in its spiritual revelation of the text, is speaking about a divine, perfect marriage, a union that is a holy celebration that will take place with all who have made Jesus Christ their Lord and Savior. In this perfect marriage and union, the mother of Jesus is present, and so is Jesus, the Living Word of God.

As a side note, the Holy Spirit brings to mind that you become one with the person to whomsoever you join yourself. That is why it is of the utmost importance for all of humanity to unite to God in Christ Jesus, because there is no other way that one can be counted as righteous to become a member of Christ's body and become a mother and womb to Him.

You might be asking yourself, *"How can I be a mother to Jesus? Wasn't Mary, the mother of Jesus?"* Yes, Mary was the mother of Jesus, the child, the Word made flesh, but why? Is she the only mother of Jesus? The religions of men that mixed a Greco-Roman religion, Christianity, philosophies, and were carnal, all after Jesus' ascending into Heaven, made Mary out to be something above Jesus. But Mary was only a channel through whom God used to fulfill His purpose. So the answer to Mary being the mother of Jesus is both "yes" and "no."

Let me explain further. Jesus made it clear that Mary was not to be His only mother. He teaches us who His mother in the Word of God is according to **Mark 3:35,** *"For whosoever shall do the will of God, the same is my brother, and my sister, and mother.* In **Luke 8:21**, Jesus, the Messiah, is speaking and says, *"My mother and my brethren are these which hear the word of God, and do it."*

This *"**hearing the word of God, and doing it**"* is why Mary became the mother of Jesus to bring Him into the world in flesh and blood. In **Luke 1:37-38**, it says, *"For with God nothing shall be impossible."* It was just that with Mary. Mary said, *"Behold the handmaid of the Lord; be it unto me according to thy word. And the angel departed from her."* **Mary heard the Word of God from the messenger, the Angel Gabriel, and as she heard the Will of God. She decided to believe the divine Word of God and not reject it. She then carried out the will of God by receiving it and taking action by speaking what she believed.** Mary declared, *"Be it unto me according to thy word."* Because of this, the Holy Spirit came upon her and deposited the seed, the Word of the Living God, that is Jesus. She then cultivated the seed, nurtured the seed, and aligned herself in the mother's position by believing the seed of the Living Word in her.

Even though she had no intercourse with a man, Mary allowed the Word of God to produce what God had spoken into her, by which He impregnated her. By her faith in God, it took form until, eventually, it was no longer in seed form. The Word of God began to take shape in her, and baby Jesus began to kick her being in her womb. Let me encourage some of you today that if God spoke into you a divine seed, do not abort it by your unbelief or what others might say about you. Instead, know that it will not be long before the seed begins to develop. The vision, the dream, and the promise will start to kick you until it becomes evident to others that what you have in you is a divine Child of God. That is Jesus, the Messiah, manifesting Himself once again as the Living Word. These actions of faith qualify any believer, as it did Mary, to receive from God the manifestation of the divine child we as believers have the privilege to birth for the Glory of God.

Please do not ignore that **those who do God's will (The Mother)** cause **the Verb (Jesus)** to manifest Himself no matter where they are. They allow God to intervene. **They petition God in Jesus' name, motivated by love and compassion, when others suffer shame. They yield to God and allow Him to manifest His Living Word, His promises, and the laws of His Kingdom.** The Mother of Jesus, meaning those who do the will of the Father, are the channel in which the river of life will flow through and bring unity in the family between God the Father and His children —to manifest in this natural, visible world the divine promise of God, that is, **the Verb—Jesus Messiah—the Word of God in action.**

Brothers and sisters, God is looking for you to be the Mother, to take His Word and do it, bringing about His will even when no one else believes that it is in you. If God said it and you have faith, it is so, which fills me with great joy. First, to know that spiritually speaking, God causes me to become His spiritual womb in which His Word takes form. Second, God can produce in and through me from the supernatural, eternal realm to the visible, natural realm.

The Word Present to Become One with You

John 2:2
"And both Jesus was called, and his disciples, to the marriage."

If there is a marriage, there is also a marriage reception that Jesus and His disciples attended. The text now shows us what takes place after the ceremony of that wedding. Anyone who has experienced being in a wedding ceremony knows that the word of God, who is Jesus and his followers, and the minister are vital to the ceremony. The minister joins the couple together in Holy Matrimony by way of the Word of God. The followers of the Word of God bear witness to this sacred union.

However, at the reception, the Minister who joined them is often ignored and put aside. The one who brought **the Word of God—Life** and joined them together by the Word of God is forgotten and marginalized. After this, those who are without a relationship with God begin the party that involves drinking wine, dancing, talking, and acting out. More drinking occurs, and they indulge in the flesh, seeking to have a good time.

This type of carnal celebration profits nothing because once it is over, it leads to shame and emptiness. Remember that marriage is a sacrament and should be treated as such. Many couples often get married, invoking God's blessing, then put the Word of God aside and are left with a form of life that is stained with shame and discontent. A married couple must ensure not to fall into this lifeless marriage. By keeping God and His Word as the absolute authority in the marriage, one will see that when there are differences of opinion, a married couple can put both views aside. Then, stand upon the Word of God that will never steer a marriage wrong if the couple has faith in God's Word.

So, in **John 2:2**, Jesus is present. The disciples, followers of Jesus, are present, and those who do the will of God the Father and have the ability to identify a lifeless environment —the mother, are present upon the earth. They were at a fully blown-out party, but did not feel inferior to the environment. Notice also that Jesus did not run out. Instead, He waited among them because He was confident in knowing who He is, and as believers in Christ Jesus, we must do the same. As we have accepted Jesus in our hearts, He can now, through us, enter into this world, which has a form of life that is dead with shame. He can manifest Himself to all of us if we would simply obey His Word at all times. Through love and by God's amazing grace through Christ Jesus, we can bring those who are in shame out of their spiritual wasteland. In short, wedding guests should celebrate the marriage, but celebrate it in a manner that is in keeping with the special importance God gives to a marriage. That importance is the spiritual and physical union of two of His children.

The Holy Spirit in this text also shows me how we are invited to a divine marriage, and we are not to take that lightly. We must take it as the divine privilege that it is, and we must be ready to attend the marriage in the garments of holiness. Garments that God has provided for us through the Blood of Y'shua, who is Jesus the Messiah—the King of kings and Lord of lords. **Matthew 22:1-14** declares that we are called to invite all people, whether good or bad, to the divine union. The Lord alone will judge their garments, whether of faith and righteousness in Christ Jesus, or if that of their works, in which they will be cast out into outer darkness. Please note that the King of kings, Jesus, calls all people His friends until they, of their own rebellion, reject His goodness.

Another example of this is found in **Matthew 25:1-13**. Here it speaks of ten virgins, five that were prepared and had oil for their lamps, so when the Lord came, they went with Him, but the other five had no oil, and when they knocked on the door and said, "Lord, we went to get oil." This oil means the life of the Spirit. **Jesus declared unto them in verse 13**, "*I know you not.*" So, in all of this, we must be ready, for no one knows the time or the hour in which He will come, and we who have been called to this amazing marriage must be found ready. We must also be wise in humbly obeying God and not exalting ourselves. But instead, let Him give us the position and place that He has assigned to us, lest we also pass shame (see **Luke 14:7-14**).

The Mother of Jesus Is Gifted to Discern

John 2:3
"*And when they wanted wine, the mother of Jesus saith unto him, They have no wine.*"

There is a problem here; they are in want of wine in this celebration. **The wine represents joy, the fruit of life, the Vine that humanity is in want of, and His name is the I AM, Y'shua—Jesus the Messiah!** Notice that the Mother who does the will of God is the one who discerns the environment and declares to the Living Word that these people have no wine. As believers, we have been given by God the ability to discern where there is no life. We also have the privilege to petition through the Living Word of God to supply the very life that humanity seeks, which is Jesus Christ.

Now, the people at this wedding celebration were clueless that there was no wine. To the people, everything was fine. They had wine "life," but they could not see the reality of the problem in their environment because they were kept in the dark that there was no wine and therefore, were without life. They apparently had life in their own eyes, just like the world today, which has an appearance of life.

They say, "I live a respectable life, I don't bother or harm anyone, I am good according to society and my own standards," but they do not realize that without God, there is no life, only death. They cannot discern their lifeless condition because the enemy, Satan, has kept them in the dark.

The only ones who can identify if true life is present are those who do the will of God the Father and the mother of the Word of the Living God through Jesus Christ. He gives us His knowledge and wisdom as believers to continue being the channel through which the Life of God can touch the people in the world today. You see, when Jesus Christ walked the earth, it was of great shame and embarrassment to run out of wine in such a union and celebration. The reason? It symbolized that to which one was joining themselves, whether an abundance of Life or want. Here, the mercy of God is so great that He reaches out to help those with an appearance of life because they are ignorant of the condition into which the enemy deceives them. So God loves humanity first, even while many still choose a life of sin.

Operating by Faith to Get Results

John 2:4-5
"Jesus saith unto her, Woman, what have I to do with thee? mine hour is not yet come. 5 His mother saith unto the servants, Whatsoever he saith unto you, do it."

One might ask, Why is Jesus responding this way? Here, the mother reaches out to Jesus to help meet this need, and he declares that His hour or time has not yet come. Please learn this and **notice the response of the mother (those that do the will of God);** she overrides time with her faith and says to the servants, "***Whatever He tells you to do, do it.***" This action is essential because **even when the hour or time is not right, it will happen if you have faith in God's**

word and obey His laws and principles. Know that as you decree, speaking in line with the Word of God, Jesus will manifest His Word, and you will see Jesus manifest the best Wine: His life, joy, healing, and prosperity **because He is the Vine.**

We must do the same as believers. By the law of faith in God's Word, we can override the law of the natural time as we have the confidence of God's Word manifesting before us, and follow Mary's example when the Angel Gabriel first came to her. Mary, by Faith, received the seed of the word of God in her womb. Mary knew she could believe that God would meet this need because of what God had spoken to her concerning Jesus. Jesus is the goodwill of God toward all men, and He was among them, and the good news is He is still among us who believe in Him.

Mary, the mother of Jesus, used the same law of Faith in her pregnancy and her request to Jesus for more wine. Remember, the Word of God teaches that **Faith is in the present, not the future (Hebrews 11:1).** The law of Faith can override the law of time. Faith says, "**Everything that God says I have through Jesus Christ, I have it now. I am not waiting to obtain it; it has been obtained already, and I have it. My Faith is founded upon the Word of God, which is sown as a seed in my spiritual womb, where it is being formed and grows, even though others cannot see it. By Faith, I know it is there, and even though others do not know it or can feel it, I do, and I feel it kicking inside me, and I know it is in my spiritual womb, which carries this child of God. His Word will not abort in me.**"

Mary said all that He tells you to do, do it, because she knew that if you stand upon the Word of God in faith, Jesus, who is the Living Word, will manifest what you believe Him to bring to pass. I may not understand or know exactly how He is going to do it, but one thing I know is, I have it, and HE WILL DO IT.   As the mother is motivated by love, she will operate in true faith by standing firm upon the covenant of God's Word.

In **Galatians 5:6**, it says *faith works by love*, this being the motive of those who do the will of God the Father. To ensure that Jesus will manifest His Word, not sometimes, or even now and then, but all the time. By this same motive of love and faith that works through God's Word, we must continue as believers to instruct others to do all that Jesus has taught us to do. That is to do the will of our Heavenly Father.

Religion Never the Intent for Humanity

All that fallen men ever accomplished is injustice, motivated by power and greed. What is considered progress and advancement is rooted and recorded forever in history in abuse and sin, including religious politics and wars. The only hope for humanity is that of the only true Savior, Jesus the Messiah, the Word of God made flesh, to rescue them from their sinful nature. This sinful nature of humanity wraps them up, to walk with no sight of true justice, doomed to eternal death unless they repent and embrace the gift of God to save them through Jesus Christ.

Although some have argued that those born in different cultures cannot be expected to forsake their religions completely, I would challenge their understanding. You see, religions, regardless of Hindu, Buddhist, Jewish, Catholic, Pentecostal, Lutheran, or any of the others that exist, were never God's intent for humanity. To this day, I can assure you that none of the carnally minded religions made by humanity, regardless of their quoting scriptures in the Bible, are God's intent for the human race. God is Spirit, and Spirit does not agree with the carnal mind that dominates fallen humanity.

Instead, God, who is a Spirit and the only definition of absolute Truth, seeks those who worship Him in Spirit and Truth.

Therefore, when you remove the religions made up of humanity. Then, establish the definition of God as Jesus Christ, the Word made flesh, the Son of God, revealing Spirit God for us incarnated (John 4:24). Then, you can ask all people, regardless of their culture and religious beliefs, if they desire to be free of the lies of evil by the absolute Truth that can only come from God, who is a Spirit. Further, one can ask any person if they desire the Way, the Truth, and Life in which Jesus requested God the Father to sanctify all that would believe that He was the Son of God to be saved and sanctified through Him (**John 14:6, and John 17:17**). Thus, by removing the religious views of fallen humanity about God and pointing them to seek Truth, one can rest assured if they ever come to the Truth, God's Living Word. They will end up having to embrace Yeshua-Jesus, which means Yahweh Saves through the anointed one who is the Truth. Or they will reject the Truth and abide by their lies.

To illustrate this point further, look at what the Word of God states in **John 2:6**, *"And there were set there, <u>six</u> waterpots of stone after the manner of the purifying of the Jews, containing two or three firkins apiece."* <u>Notably, the number **six** is the number of humanity; the water-pots of stone represent mankind made in the image and likeness of God.</u> **God created mankind to have the life of His Holy Spirit, which is represented by water.** The scripture here says these water pots of stone were being used after the manner of "*the purifying of the Jews.*" This meant they were being used for man-made religious traditions. The water pots contained two to three firkins apiece, which speaks to a perfect testimony. **To no surprise, the water pots were empty, and I am submitting to you that many people's lives, even in local congregations, regardless of their religion, are like these water pots, being used for**

traditions and religious acts made up by men, but they have no life of the Spirit of God in them.

Do not allow this to be you! Service to God is not enough. It is serving that is out of the heart and motive of worship in the Spirit of God, which is love demonstrated by obedience to His Word that brings about a pleasant aroma before God. You see, you can attend church services. Serve in a gathering place and become busy doing things that appear spiritual on the outside. Still, inwardly in your heart, you can be as carnal as the unbeliever who openly blasphemes God. You can have an appearance that you are alive, but have no life in you. Remember, God weighs and sees the heart of man.

In **I Peter 2:4-5**, it says, "*To whom coming, as unto a living stone, disallowed indeed of men, but chosen of God, and precious, 5 Ye also, as lively stones, are built up a spiritual house, an holy priesthood, to offer up spiritual sacrifices, acceptable to God by Jesus Christ.*" We are to be **living stones**, but how can a stone be alive? Only if God is abiding in that stone with the substance of life. It says that the water-pots of stone had a capacity of two to three firkins apiece: that speaks of humanity's purpose, which is to give a perfect testimony of the Living God. However, as mentioned before, the water-pots of stone were empty.

This emptiness is the condition and state of the world; for all that do not have Jesus the Messiah as their Lord and Savior in their lives—they are water-pots of stone, which have the capacity to receive **water (Life of the Spirit of God)** that they would be living testimonies of the One True God and that is the purpose for which they were created. Due to traditions and the deceptive methods of men whose rituals give them a form of godliness but deny the Power and True life of God, they find themselves empty. People without God try to commit acts of kindness to justify their selfish actions and agendas. However, they are still empty and unfulfilled because they continue in a state of carnal desires that is enmity with the Spirit of God's life.

Life, God's True Desire
For All Humanity

John 2:7 (KJV)
*"Jesus saith unto them, **Fill the waterpots with water.** And they filled them up to the brim."*

The Living Word (Jesus) instructs those who serve and obey Him. Jesus declares to His people who believe and serve Him to fill the empty water-pots of stone with the Holy Spirit's life flowing through them. In other words, fill the lives of the people, created in the image and likeness of God, with real-life through the Gospel of Jesus the Messiah. Jesus has provided the Spirit-Life to all flesh who would believe in Him and gives those who serve the responsibility to fill the water-pots. Now Jesus said, "***Fill them,***" and those who served at this feast filled them up to the brim. As the body of Christ, we, the Church of the Lord Jesus Christ, must ensure we take the same actions to fill people up to the brim. Too often, many who preach the Good News of salvation fill people's lives partially with the Good News of the Gospel. This partial good news leaves many of our brothers and sisters saved but still in want. Saved but without the gifts of the Holy Spirit operating through them. Saved and making it to heaven but having no understanding of their purpose while in this world, believers in Christ that struggle with the same issues as those in the world.

As those entrusted by God to lead people, we must not limit the growth and development of those we lead. You see, God gave us the privilege to be the channel through which the river of life will flow, and He has an unlimited supply. We must never limit God, and we must passionately pursue to manifest the Kingdom of God just like Jesus. You will only grow to the degree you believe, so if all you teach and believe is salvation, then that is all the people will get. However, suppose you believe in salvation, healing, prosperity, deliverance, and walking with God "*on earth as it is in heaven*" without limits. In that case, that is what you and those you lead will get. We must believe that God will do what He promised. Do not settle for anything less than Jesus, the Messiah, who died on the cross to make us joint heirs with Him. It takes being filled to the brim and overflowing to demonstrate the Kingdom of God to a world that is seeking real life and has to settle for an appearance of life. All because they have yet to come across believers who are filled to the brim.

John 2:8
"And he saith unto them, Draw out now, and bear unto the governor of the feast. And they bare it."

Jesus gives the command, *"Draw out now,"* take the new life I have made you a dispenser of, and take it to the governor of the feast. The *governor of the feast* is defined in the **Strong Concordance Greek#755 as *the director of entertainment.*** Jesus is sending us filled with this new wine to those in authority. According to the Word of God, **this New Wine is the BEST WINE because it is True Life**. We are sent to those who are directors of their entertainment, people seeking the pleasures and lust of the mortal flesh for relief from the emptiness produced by a world whose inspiration is the king of darkness and death, the enemy of God. However, God respects humanity's free will to choose between real life and what we have had to settle for, which is an appearance of life that leaves people empty. Now, according to those who have yet to drink this new wine, they go about saying all is well: "I don't hurt anyone, I am living the moment, I only have one life to live." Yet they wake up in regret, in pain, or having caused pain, abused by someone who took advantage of them. Or even worse, they take the life of someone because they gave themselves over to be entirely under the influence of darkness.

This evil brought about by fallen humanity, inspired by Satan, is why it is of extreme importance for the members of the body of Christ to rediscover and be restored to their new identity as sons and daughters of God. We are called by God and chosen to take this real life to the people who have authority over their lives so that they might choose God and be restored to who God created them to be. We take the **New Wine (True Life)** for them to taste. As they experience that the Lord is good, nothing they drink or experience in the world of darkness will compare to Him. The best life is reserved for all who are born again in the Spirit. The dispensation of Grace in which real life and joy remain constant and forever is now our portion.

> When the ruler of the feast had tasted the water that was made wine, and knew not whence it was: (but the servants which drew the water knew;) the governor of the feast called the bridegroom, And saith unto him, Every man at the beginning doth set forth good wine; and when men have well drunk, then that which is worse: but thou hast kept the good wine until now. (**John 2:9-10**)

When those who hear and do the will of God go forth and serve the Living Word of God to the directors of their own entertainment, and by having the substance of this real-life in them, giving them a taste of it, they will notice that having Jesus the Messiah and His Holy Spirit is real LIFE. They will recognize that the Best Wine that Jesus gives us to dispense is far better than anything the world has, and because of this, they will call for the bridegroom. Now the question arises: what have you been serving the people who have yet to know God? Is it the New Wine or a watered-down, fake imitation called the religion of men and women? If anyone indeed drinks this new wine, no matter who they are and what they have experienced, they will realize that Jesus is the way, the truth, and the life. They will be calling for Him.

My brothers and sisters, Church of the Lord Jesus Christ, the Bridegroom has saved the best wine for last. He is calling us to serve it throughout the whole world; in this dispensation of Grace, we have been privileged to have been born into it for His Glory. In this dispensation, we are porters of the true life, this best wine that is Jesus-Y'shua the Messiah. In this natural time, we have been commissioned. We are to go into the entire world and have them taste this best wine, and as they taste it, the same thing that happened to us will happen to them. They will choose to be born again in the Spirit of God and know that nothing that exists compares to **Jesus, the I AM,** who fills us with His Holy Spirit, His fire, and power. Jesus Christ, the I AM, is our Salvation, Prosperity, Healing, Holiness, Miracles, Peace, Light, Wine, Vine, Joy, Author, and Finisher of our Faith. **He is True Life**.

John 2:11
"This beginning of miracles did Jesus in Cana of Galilee, and manifested forth his glory; and his disciples believed on him."

Hebrews 13:8
"Jesus (Y'shua) the Messiah is the same yesterday, today, and forever."

Acts 10:38 (KJV)
"How God anointed Jesus of Nazareth with the Holy Ghost and with power: who went about doing good and healing all that were oppressed of the devil; for God was with him."

Jesus is still in the business of saving lives, delivering them from sin, and demonstrating His Kingdom power. Jesus continues to leave all humanity in awe of Him through us who believe and obey His Word. Through faith in Jesus' name, the Grace of God is that believers in Christ are water-pots of stone that have come to life with His wine, that can become all things pertaining to life and godliness to all people. He has sent us out into the world, not to fit in or become like them, but rather to be the rest they seek. I am sent to tell you this day that, as you embrace that God has made you one of His manifested sons upon the earth, the new wine of healing, joy, love, rest, prosperity, and peace flows through you. All that He is has been deposited in us, as believers, to serve all who are thirsty so that they would thirst no more. God is still ensuring that His Word does not return to Him void. God continually confirms to us who believe that He still brings forth signs and wonders of His glory. All to confirm what the whole world knows, that the tomb of God's Son is empty, and Jesus the Messiah is Alive!

What Mind Will You Choose?

Those who are not believers worry about what they shall eat and drink. They are of a doubtful mind, but this cannot be you. **Luke 12:29** declares, "*And seek not ye what ye shall eat, or what ye shall drink, **neither be ye of doubtful mind**.*" If you have been of a **doubtful mind**, repent and be of the mind and mindset of Christ, that is of God.

People, it is a choice, a decision of what mind you will choose to have and impart to others. You will either put evil in people's minds or righteousness. It is in your hands, life or death. Choose to put life. Do not be like the wicked, who love to divide people and cause havoc, strife, gossip, and envy. Evil influences carnal people to destroy what God intended for all humanity to have: an abundance of life. The scripture in **Acts 14:2** tells us, "*But **the unbelieving** Jews stirred up the Gentiles, **and made their minds evil affected against the brethren**.*" We must ensure we are not producing evil, which is of the old nature of those without Christ Jesus.

The believer must be of **a readiness of mind,** willing to receive instruction and verify it by the foundation of the Word and the guidance of the Holy Spirit, to ensure that what is received aligns with the mind and mindset of Christ.

These were more noble than those in Thessalonica, in that **they received the word with all readiness of mind**, and searched the scriptures daily, whether those things were so. (**Acts 17:11**)

For if there be first a willing mind, it is accepted according to that a man hath, and not according to that he hath not. (**II Corinthians 8:12**)

Afterward, the believer must act on the instructions received from the Holy Spirit, once they confirm through the Word that it was indeed God speaking and not the carnal mind.

Nevertheless, the wicked that reject God are, by choice, given into **a reprobate mind** that becomes shameless and chooses damnation. **Romans 1:28** "*And even as they did not like to retain God in their knowledge, God gave them over to **a reprobate mind**, to do those things which are not convenient;*" Please note that they made a choice for themselves, and it was not God who decided for them. God gives them over to a reprobate mind because they choose to walk on in darkness by not wanting God's knowledge and counsel.

An example of this is a good parent giving a child good advice to take a path that will bring blessings, but the child chooses to ignore the parent's guidance and knowledge, ultimately suffering in a cold and dark world. **Philippians 3:19** "*Whose end is destruction, whose God is their belly, and whose glory is in their shame, who mind earthly things.*" Minding only earthly things will cause a person to think counterfeit thoughts, which have the appearance of being alive and genuine but are far from it. **Ephesians 2:3** declares, "*Among whom also we all had our conversation in times past in the lusts of our flesh, fulfilling the desires of the flesh and of the mind; and were by nature the children of wrath, even as others.*" **The unbeliever fulfills the desires of the flesh with a <u>Lustful</u> Mind and Mindset!** And by nature are children of wrath and destruction; that's why everything always falls apart for the unbeliever.

It is easy to identify what mind you are choosing or have chosen. **What are you thinking about? Is it God, His Word, and His life? Or is it the sinful desires of this world, having to do with only natural earthly things known as a Carnal Mind that are selfish and vain?** Romans 8:5-7, *"For they that are after the flesh do mind the things of the flesh; but they that are after the Spirit the things of the Spirit. For to be carnally minded is death; but to be spiritually minded is life and peace. Because the carnal mind is enmity against God: for it is not subject to the law of God, neither indeed can be."* **Do not be of a mind and mindset full of vanity—imagining ungodly things.** Thinking it is all about you, and as long as you get what you want, nothing else matters. The Bible says in **Ephesians 4:17** *"This I say therefore, and testify in the Lord, that ye henceforth walk not as other Gentiles walk, in the vanity of their mind."* Those who choose to focus on fleshly worldly things are walking in vanity.

The mind of the Spirit is the mind of Christ, which is the will of God and brings forth Heaven's best upon those who abide in it. The Bible states, *"And he that searcheth the hearts knoweth what is the mind of the Spirit, because he maketh intercession for the saints according to the will of God* (**Romans 8:27**)." If you decide to focus on the Spirit, you will be able to walk and live in God's perfect will in which the Holy Spirit has interceded for you that will cause every decision you make to be for your good. Even when it appears that what you have done was a mistake, if you live in the Spirit, you can rest assured that the perfect intercession of the Spirit has already anticipated and resolved for your good the outcome of what you are going through.

The mindset of Christ is one that empowers, encourages others, and gives honor. *'Let nothing be done through strife or vainglory; but in lowliness of mind let each esteem other* *better than themselves* **(Philippians 2:3)**." We need to become the doers of this Word to truly see the Glory of God, which He chooses to express through every one of His members in the unique way of His design.

The mindset of Christ is *one of unity and love toward one another.*

> Fulfil ye my joy, that ye **be likeminded, having the same love, being of one accord, of one mind**. **(Philippians 2:2)**

> That ye may **with one mind and one mouth glorify God,** even the Father of our Lord Jesus Christ. **(Romans 15:6)**

The body of Christ is to speak out of one mind and be unified, loving God and one another, and glorifying God.

However, you cannot have the mind of Christ without accepting Christ first. You are alone in darkness without Him, but once you embrace Christ Jesus, you have been reconciled to live in total victory. To live in victory, you must have the mindset of Christ that leads you to respond by speaking the words of the good treasure in your heart (Mind), which is the Word of God, responding with the mindset of Christ. **Luke 6:45** says, "*A good man out of the good treasure of his heart bringeth forth that which is good; and an evil man out of the evil treasure of his heart bringeth forth that which is evil: for of the abundance of the **heart-(Mind)** his mouth speaketh.*" In this passage of scripture referencing the Strong's Concordance, the words *"heart"* and *"mind"* are side by side as the definitions of the original Greek word translated into English.

Do not be of a blinded mind that the enemy brings upon those who do not believe the Word of God, as they rely only on the traditions and religious acts of self-righteousness to attempt to save themselves. Read the following scriptures about this:

> But **their minds were blinded**: for until this day remaineth the same vail untaken away in the reading of the Old Testament; which veil is done away in Christ (**II Corinthians 3:14**). In whom **the god of this world hath blinded the minds of them which believe not**, lest the light of the glorious gospel of Christ, who is the image of God, should shine unto them (**II Corinthians 4:4**). And you, that were sometime **alienated and enemies in your mind by wicked works,** yet now hath he reconciled (**Colossians 1:21**).

Those blinded by Satan, the god of this world, can choose not to remain blind by choosing the light of the gospel of Jesus Christ and believing in his redemptive work on their behalf.

Remember that through Christ, you now have His mind and mentality. Allow Him to respond through you. Stop allowing Satan to deprive you of what God has blessed and released to you.

Be of humbleness of mind; **Colossians 3:12** clearly instructs us, saying, *"Put on therefore, as the elect of God, holy and beloved, bowels of mercies, kindness, **humbleness of mind**, meekness, longsuffering;"* this is an individual who obeys God at all times and rejects selfishness. A person who is not self-governed but instead yields to the leading of the Holy Spirit, ready to carry out and demonstrate God's command in love.

Christ's mindset responds with Holiness, knowing, as the elect of God, how to give out mercies and kindness without boosting oneself but giving Glory to God who is Holy. **The mindset of Christ is what will allow all believers to agree, working in unity to glorify His name.**

Now I beseech you, brethren, by the name of our Lord Jesus Christ, that ye all speak the same thing, and that there be no divisions among you; but that ye be **perfectly joined together in the same mind** and in the same judgment. (**I Corinthians 1:10**)

But I fear, lest by any means, as the serpent beguiled Eve through his subtlety, so **your minds should be corrupted from the simplicity** that is in Christ. (**II Corinthians 11:3**)

People of God, this is not hard or complex. If Christ said it, do it. **Otherwise, the enemy can deceive you once you question whether God really has your best interests at heart.**

Christ's Mind and Mindset are of a peaceful mind for you. This mindset is not moved by the circumstances that surround the naturally seen realm. It knows zero defeat and is completely confident in the ability of God, our Father, who has granted us perfect peace no matter what is happening. To abide in a peaceful mind, we must continually stay focused on God. Knowing He is for us and cares for us to the degree that there is no way, no how we will be defeated, for He is Mighty in battle on our behalf. It is as with David against Goliath. Saul and all of Israel's army were shaken in their minds, troubled by the words of the giant who was but an ant compared to the God of Israel in whom David was confident.

The covenant in which David had and trusted in God to cut the giant's head off teaches us that we must be confident in the new covenant we have through Jesus Christ to cut the giant's head off in our lives and those around us. So walk confidently and pay no attention to words of doubt sent to make you afraid, but rather walk in the revelation of the One, Jesus our Lord, who paid the price for our total success and victory, both now and in the world to come.

The Word of God teaches us not to worry:

> And **the peace of God**, which passeth all understanding, **shall keep your hearts and minds** through Christ Jesus. [**Philippians 4:7**)
> Thou wilt keep him **in perfect peace, whose mind is stayed on thee**: because he trusteth in thee. (**Isaiah 26:3**)
> That ye **be not soon shaken in mind,** or be troubled, neither by spirit, nor by word, nor by letter as from us, as that the day of Christ is at hand. (**II Thessalonians 2:2**)
> Wherefore **gird up the loins of your mind**, be sober, and hope to the end for the grace that is to be brought unto you at the revelation of Jesus Christ; (**I Peter 1:13**)

God is always for us, and He affirms us. **Only believe and strengthen your mind** and think on the Holy Spirit, who gives hope, faith, and peace by God's unmerited favor manifested to you by knowing that all Jesus Christ has accomplished is for our benefit.

Moreover, the Word teaches us not to rely on our way of thinking. **Romans 12:16** declares, *"Be of the same mind one toward another. Mind not high things, but condescend to men of low estate. **Be not wise in your own conceits.**"*

> Only let your conversation be as it becometh the gospel of Christ: that whether I come and see you, or else be absent, I may hear of your affairs, that ye stand fast in one spirit, **with one mind** striving together for the faith of the gospel; (**Philippians 1:27**)

Listen, my brothers and sisters, it is time to renounce our own intelligence and take on the intelligence of the Supreme One. The wisest thing a person can do is to obey God. He created all things, including what we call the intellect.

Don't be tricked by a fleshly mind. Colossians 2:18 declares, "*Let no man beguile you of your reward in a voluntary humility and worshipping of angels, intruding into those things which he hath not seen, **vainly puffed up by his fleshly mind.**" Many, having a fleshly mind, have gone after their own deity in an attempt to have things their way as opposed to God's. They then seduce others into believing like them to continue in their lust; the carnal intellectual institutions are examples of this. So, be on guard and do not allow yourself to become a victim of those with a fleshly mind.

Don't be of a Faint Mind. In **Hebrews 12:3,** it states, "*For consider him that endured such contradiction of sinners against himself, **lest ye be wearied and faint in your minds.**" We must learn not to entertain all the contradictions of people who are without God. The more you allow negative thoughts, the bigger the negative voice gets in you to the point where it can wear you out. Do not entertain negative thoughts; instead, cast them down and focus on Christ Jesus' thoughts, which are His Word.

Remember, now you are of a Pure Mind in Christ Jesus. In **II Peter 3:1,** "*This second epistle, beloved, I now write unto you; in both which **I stir up your pure minds by way of remembrance:**" Here, Peter is used by God to remind us that **we have a pure mind, which is of God that must be stirred up on purpose.** Live in this mind by continually stirring it by the Word of God. How? The Holy Spirit reminds us of the Word and puts it in our minds. **John 14:26** says, "*But the Comforter, which is the Holy Ghost, whom the Father will send in my name, he shall teach you all things, and bring all things to your remembrance, whatsoever I have said unto you.*" Make sure you spend time getting to know the voice of the Holy Spirit, who will remind you what Jesus has said.

What You Speak Exposes Your Mind

Do not speak perversely; it is an indicator of **a corrupt mind** rooted in Satan himself. In **I Timothy 6:5**, we are told, *"Perverse disputings of **men of corrupt minds, and destitute of the truth, supposing that gain is godliness**: from such withdraw thyself."* The word perversion is twisting words of Truth; this is what Satan used by his nature, speaking through the serpent in the Garden of Eden to Eve (Woman).

The father of perversion is Satan, who will do anything and say anything to get you away from the Truth and gain you by seducing you to twist your words to acquire things. Be bold against the enemy and take vengeance upon him by obeying God. Even if you have missed it in the past, repent, have a change of mind, and cease to do it anymore. The Word of God speaks about two sorcerers named Jannes and Jambres, who served Pharaoh in Moses's time. **II Timothy 3:8, "*Now as Jannes and Jambres withstood Moses, so do these also resist the truth: men of corrupt minds, reprobate concerning the faith.*"** They took a truth about the spirit world and twisted it to operate in the occult. This twisting of the truth is of those who have a form and manifestation of power and godliness for gain, but deny the power of the Most High God.

The Sound Mind of God's Spirit is Supernatural. What we, in the natural, would call supernatural is now the sound mind of God's Spirit in us. **II Timothy 1:7** states, *"For God hath not given us the spirit of fear; but of power, and of love, and **of a sound mind.**"* So, as we no longer have a spirit of fear and limitation but one of omnipotent power, love, and God's supernatural sound mind, we can now move confidently in our new sober mind, which is of God. The Word of God says to us in **Titus 2:6**, *"Young men likewise exhort to **be sober minded.**"* According to the will of God, being of a **sober mind means a Kingdom of God mindset**. Remember, we are no longer of this world; we are citizens of the Kingdom of Heaven. We must operate by the laws of the Kingdom of God, as we were born into it and received Jesus Christ as our Lord and Savior.

Without God, your mind and conscience are defiled. Titus 1:15, "*Unto the pure all things are pure: but unto them that are defiled and unbelieving is nothing pure; **but even their mind and conscience is defiled**.*" Please do not allow the enemy, who has deceived the whole world into thinking that drugs, sex before marriage, adultery, homosexuality, worldly wisdom, including higher education that has ignorantly rejected God and all lust alike, to be normal. Do not allow lying and deceiving people to get ahead to be the norm. Sure, we have all fallen and have sinned in many carnal ways at one point or another. But let us return to being humble and admitting our mistakes. Let us ask for forgiveness when we have wronged someone and do our part to receive God's mercy and full Grace through Jesus Christ, our Lord. Otherwise, all that will happen is that people will call what is good evil and what is evil good, see (**Isaiah 5:20**).

Again and again, we see that we are to put the Word of God in mind. **Titus 3:1** says, "*Put them in mind to be subject to principalities and powers, to obey magistrates, to be ready to every good work.*" We are to purposely put the will of God in our minds, even when it comes to following the laws of the land, so long as they are in line with what is right according to the will of God.

Do not be DOUBLE-MINDED, which means one moment for God, the next for the world. Look at what else the scriptures say about this in **James 1:8**, "*A double minded man is unstable in all his ways.*" **James 4:8,** "*Draw nigh to God, and he will draw nigh to you. Cleanse your hands, ye sinners; and **purify your hearts, ye double minded**.*" **I Peter 3:8,** "*Finally, **be ye all of one mind**, having compassion one of* *another, love as brethren, be pitiful, be courteous:"* Determine today that you will not be double-minded but rather of one mind that is of the mind and mindset of Christ.

You cannot expect to see the fullness of God's blessing and Kingdom made visible to you and through you if you are still insecure in all God has provided and promised you. Remember, without faith, it is impossible to please God. Everything you do must be with a single eye, of one mind, meaning God said it, and so it is—period!

There are no ifs or buts about it. There is no wavering saying yes, I believe, and once faced with natural pressures applied by Satan and his army, saying, "Where are you, God?" There is only absolute conviction and trust in knowing God will not fail (**Joshua 1:5**). It is already as He has promised and revealed to us through His Word and complete work at the cross through Jesus Christ, our Lord.

Once we have become of one mind with God, we will have the **suffering mind of Christ** that enables us to patiently love and help those who cannot see in the Spirit. **The suffering mind of Christ means** death to all selfish ways and to the benefits you are rightfully entitled to, for the sake of giving it freely to others to bless them. **I Peter 4:1** says, *"Forasmuch then as Christ hath suffered for us in the flesh, **arm yourselves likewise with the same mind:** for he that hath suffered in the flesh hath ceased from sin;"* **To suffer in the flesh means** not to give in to the temptation of your carnal desires but rather mortify them to help others.

We must be of a READY MIND. A mind that is not caught up in the things of the world for selfish gain but instead serves to bless others and leads them by example. The Word of God says in **I Peter 5:2,** *"Feed the flock of God, which is among you, taking the oversight thereof, not by constraint, but willingly; **not for filthy lucre, but of a ready mind;"*** Continually remember the Word, put it in your **Mind, be**

Mindful of it, and get in the Word. **II Peter 3:2**, "*That ye may be mindful of the words which were spoken before by the holy prophets, and of the commandment of us the apostles of the Lord and Saviour:*" Getting in the Word will make you of a ready mind, that will allow you to hear God by His Spirit. **Rhema, which is the spoken Word of God**, will come to you so that you may always walk in victory by being a doer of the Word of God and leading others to it.

Even Satan knows that those of the antichrist must agree and be of one mind to do anything. The principle here is not to be of the mind of Evil that is of Satan, but to be one with the Mind of Christ and His Mindset to attack and destroy the Devil's works in Jesus' name. **Revelation 17:13** mentions that these (Satan and those of the antichrist) "*Have one mind, and shall give their power and strength unto the beast.*" Remember that a Kingdom divided against itself cannot stand (see **Luke 11:17**). Satan and all evil are very aware of this principle. We, the Body of Christ, must also be aware and do the same to manifest God's will on earth as it is in Heaven. **We must be one.**

Even so, this oneness in unity can only manifest in the body of Christ by the Holy Spirit as each member of the Church willfully yields to Him as in the day of Pentecost (**Acts 2**). If the Church welcomes the Holy Spirit in unity and the Holy Spirit is present in power, this oneness remains in harmony. Still, if any member of the Church resorts to worldly wisdom and sense-based knowledge, a sense of superiority will resurface and cause discord, because every member of the body of Christ can still choose to walk in the Spirit or the lustful ways of the flesh. An example of this is after Peter witnessed the Holy Spirit move among the Gentiles (**Acts 10**), he was later confronted by Paul the Apostle when Peter, being among the Jewish believers, withdrew himself from the Gentiles (**Galatians 2:11-21**). Therefore, to end disunity in the Church and be of one mind and voice, each member must remain walking in the Spirit.

"Restoring Mankind's True Identity"

CHAPTER FIVE

Repairing your Mind by the Word of God

Repairing Your Mind by the Word Of God

The Body of Christ must be united in MIND and operating with the MINDSET of Christ as its own because it is one body. It is a choice every member of the Body of Christ must make to allow us to be what God has made us. It states in **II Corinthians 13:11**, *"Finally, brethren, farewell. Be perfect, be of good comfort, **be of one mind**, live in peace; and the God of love and peace shall be with you."* **God's command is to be of one mind**, and a decision to believe and obey is all it takes for that to manifest upon the earth.

In **Genesis 2:4**, when God made the heavens and the earth, He created them and finished them "before" it was manifested in the visible realm. To begin restoring our mind in our soul and to operate as one with the Mind of Christ, we must have an understanding of this process. Furthermore, **Genesis 2:5-14** shows how God fully supplied and granted every need and desire man and woman would have or want: life, food, gold, and companionship. Everything is already provided for us. We now have the privilege of discovering it by the substance of faith as we renew our minds.

Romans 12:2 *"And be not conformed to this world: but be ye transformed by the renewing of your mind, that ye may prove what is that good, and acceptable, and perfect, will of God."*

The word **renew** means;

> to renovate, to restore to a former state or a good state after decay or depravation; to rebuild; to repair. To re-establish, confirm, to make again, to revive, to make new. (Webster)

Did you know that, as children of God and as His manifested sons upon the earth, it is our duty by His Spirit in us to repair and rebuild the old, wasted, desolated places? Well, it is, and this will only be possible as we are renewed inside out.

> And they shall build the old wastes, they shall raise up the former desolations, and they shall repair the waste cities, the desolations of many generations. And strangers shall stand and feed your flocks, and the sons of the alien shall be your plowmen and your vinedressers. But ye shall be named the Priests of the LORD: men shall call you the Ministers of our God: ye shall eat the riches of the Gentiles, and in their glory shall ye boast yourselves. For your shame ye shall have double; and for confusion they shall rejoice in their portion: therefore in their land they shall possess the double: everlasting joy shall be unto them. (**Isaiah 61:4-7**)

To renew our minds, we must **see, look, hear, listen, meditate, speak, and roar** the word of God. We will now look at each of these words' definitions and then summarize how they fit to accomplish the mind's renewal.

> **See** means to perceive by the eye; to have knowledge of the existence and apparent quality of objects by the organs of sight, to behold; to observe: to note or notice; to know, to regard or look to, to attend as to the execution of some order, or to performance of something; to discover, understand to hear or to attend to. (Webster)

> **Look** means to direct the eye toward an object with intent of seeing it; to see or view, to apply the mind or understanding, to consider and examine, to expect.

> **Hear** means to perceive by ear; to feel on impression of sound by the proper organs; to hear sound to hear voice or words; to attend, to listen, to obey to attend

favorably to regard; to learn to approve and embrace. (Webster)

In my own words, it is to attend to and regard with submission to obey. You see, one can hear the sound but not listen and obey.

> **Listen** means to harken; to give ear; to attend closely with view to hear; to obey; to yield to advice; to follow admonition; to hear to attend.

> **Meditate** means to dwell on any thought; contemplate; to study; to turn or revolve any subject in mind; to plan by revolving in the mind; to contrive; to intend; to think on; to revolve in the mind. (Webster)

> **Roar** means to cry with a full, loud, continued sound; to bellow, as a beast, as a roaring bull or lion.

The words of Jesus come to mind when He said,

> "*Take heed therefore how ye hear: for whosoever hath, to him shall be given; and whosoever hath not, from him shall be taken even that which he seemeth to have.*" (**Luke 8:18**)

The time has come to have understanding, my beloved brothers and sisters. How you decide to pay attention and give importance to God's Word will determine whether you live as victors or victims. You see, God is no respecter of persons, but He is a respecter of faith.

Now we know that *Faith is by hearing and hearing by the Word of God*, and that requires that we **see** and **look** at the Word of God with the intent of perceiving and beholding and applying our mind to understand what God is revealing to us. At the same time, we are required to **hear, listen, and**

meditate on the sound of the impressions of the Word of God, brought to life by the Holy Spirit. The Holy Spirit will speak gentle instructions for us to attend closely to yield to God's advice and follow his admonition to think and contemplate; that we may become of One Mind and be led to **Roar the Word of God as a Lion.**

We **roar with the continual loud sound of God's very utterance**, which never changes and dominates every realm and dominion. We become the terrorists to Satan and all his forces of darkness. When the Lion Roars, because He is King and Dominator, all flee, or they will become His prey. God declares in His Word in **James 4:7**, *"Submit yourselves therefore to God. Resist the devil, and he will flee from you."*

HalleluYah—this absolutely thrills me! I just had to get up out of my chair and turn around, jumping as I saw this image, which God reveals here. All I can see is the devil and all his cohorts fleeing from anyone who will submit to God. I can see now why the devils, called Legion, cried out to my Jesus and worshiped Him when they had possessed the man in the country of the Gadarenes.

> But when he (Legion of devils in the possessed man) saw Jesus afar off, he ran and worshipped him, And cried with a loud voice, and said, what have I to do with thee, Jesus, thou Son of the most high God? I adjure thee by God, that thou torment me not. (**Mark 5:6-7**)

Glory to God! The way the legion of devils responded to Jesus is what Satan and all his cohorts will do if you ever discover all that God has made you be in Christ Jesus. The devil is defeated; he has no power over you, who are of the Most High God. Because of Jesus Christ, we are now called beloved sons of God. Praise His Holy name (see **I John 3:1**). The devil is under our feet, and so are all his workers. They bow down to the King of kings and the Lord of lords in whom we abide.

Remember, Jesus said the least in the Kingdom of God is greater than all the power of Satan and his army! HalleluYah!

Now, you must capture this image, and to do this, you must use the imagination God gave you for its original purpose. **The imagination was given and created by God to be able to see that which He promised.** <u>So long as your imagination is sowed into the Spirit and subjected to the Holy Spirit to manifest the will of God upon the earth, it is good and serves as another pair of eyes.</u> **The imagination** is used to create, from the invisible realm to the visible realm, all that God has provided. **The imagination without the Holy Spirit is perverted** and is used to make visible all that the enemy of God is, which is lust and death.

The **imagination** forms in the mind the images and pictures of God's descriptive words to give you the ability to see what others cannot see. It is a conduit of a sort used to transport from the spirit realm to the natural realm.

Imagine means:

> The formation of a mental image of something that is not perceived as real and is not present to the senses; the ability to deal resourcefully with unusual problems; the ability to form mental images of things or events; to form a notion or idea in the mind; to fancy; to cause to appear to seem. (Webster)

Notably, the devil has used humanity's imagination to bring about ungodly manifestations upon the earth that are seen daily. Some examples of the devil's expressions through societies are wars, suicides, slavery, abuse, lustful actions, and adulterous fantasies; the devil has manipulated and deceived the whole world and brings about ways of stealing, killing, and destroying all for selfish gain. God Almighty has brought about the hidden mysteries of the Kingdom of God through Jesus Christ to bring about His original purpose for making humanity in His Image and His likeness, which is to make the will of God on earth as it is in Heaven.

The Word of God declares:

> This book of the law shall not depart out of thy mouth; but thou shalt meditate therein day and night, that thou mayest observe to do according to all that is written therein: for then thou shalt make thy way prosperous, and then thou shalt have good success. Have not I commanded thee? Be strong and of a good courage; be not afraid, neither be thou dismayed: for the LORD thy God is with thee whithersoever thou goest. (**Joshua 1:8-9**)

These scriptures are a key that, if applied and obeyed, bring about an understanding of the process we have been describing. The manifestation of good success brought about in this visible realm, God's way. God's Word is to be spoken through our mouths, which releases onto the earth God's will. As we meditate on it, day and night, the Word of God creates images in our imagination, originating from the Spirit, and causes us to observe and take action, inspired by God, to make our way prosperous upon the earth for God's Glory in Jesus' name.

I heard a man of God say, "*Roar the Word of God like a lion roars.*" Out of that single statement, I went on to study what it meant to roar the Word of God. I came to understand that when we roar the Word of God like a lion, as mentioned previously, every demon and devil fears and flees from the power of the life of God, a life that dispels and destroys evil. As we do this, we always triumph in Christ and bring about the fragrance of the knowledge of God everywhere we go (see **II Corinthians 2:14**). In conclusion, **your imagination's holy purpose is to see in picture form and dream of all that God promised** of what your world could be like if you follow and obey the Word of God in Christ Jesus.

Embracing the Spirit
of God as Your Own

"But he that is joined unto the Lord is one spirit."
I Corinthians 6:17

Many people often find themselves defeated in certain areas of life, even after they have accepted Jesus as their Savior, because they have failed to make Jesus the Lord of their lives. Many are saved and going to Heaven, yet they live life defeated as unbelievers because they have not obeyed God's Word and followed Jesus Christ, as the exemplary Son, to do all that the exemplary Son has said for us to do.

The devil has deceived many into thinking that there are other ways one can live life as a son or daughter of God that do not require you to do everything the Word of God teaches you. Although you can choose to be born again, if you do not do it the way the Word of God teaches. You will never be able to fulfill all that God has intended for you to accomplish on this earth because you will still see yourself as a mere man or woman (**1Corinthians 3:3**), as opposed to seeing yourself as God has made you: a son or daughter of God, a member of the Body of Christ, **One with the Spirit of God.**

It amazes me the number of people who have ignored the process and the model Jesus Christ left us, thinking it is good to do their own thing just because they are free. Yes, we have been set free and are free, but we are free from the powers of darkness that we may walk in the fullness of the freedom of God's Kingdom and authority, to rule and reign in life as kings by the abundance of grace and the gift of righteousness we have received because of Christ Jesus our Lord.

The Word of God shows us in **I Corinthians 6:15-17** that we are members of the Body of Christ. It also indicates "who" we became one with as we joined ourselves as one. If with a

Harlot, then you are one with the Harlot; if with the Spirit of God, then one with the Spirit of God. Many today continue to move forward without knowing what manner of Spirit they are one with. **We are of the Spirit of Life.**

Many have ignored the Holy Spirit and wonder why they have gotten stuck in a routine of religious acts with no life or desire. They fall into defeat and gossip because they have gotten stagnant. If you know anything about water that gets stagnant, you would know that it begins to stink. Many born-again Christians become stuck or stagnant because they have failed to do things the way Jesus Christ did.

Jesus Christ was born of the Spirit from the moment the Holy Ghost got Mary pregnant. He then grew and increased in wisdom and favor with God and men because He was born of the Spirit. Jesus had access to drink of the Spirit as He was growing up, and as He devoted and consecrated His life of obedience to the scriptures, He was able to say no to the temptations of sin. **The reason why He was able to resist the temptations was that He was born of the Spirit.**

In this same manner, when we are born again and taken by the Holy Spirit after He has brought forth conviction of our sins, of us living outside the will of God. Once we have chosen to follow and obey the Word of God, we repent and have faith in Christ Jesus as Lord and Savior of our lives. The Holy Spirit then baptizes us into the Body of Christ, which now allows us to drink of resurrection life, and we become a new creature. At this point, we become babies as when Christ Jesus was born, having a human body, but still babies in need of the unadulterated milk of the Word of God. We needed this unadulterated milk to grow as Jesus did when he was a child (see **I Corinthians 12:13 and John 20:21-23**). If you need to recap on this matter that I just shared, you can refer back to chapter two, "**Growing in Christ to Think like God.**"

After we die with Christ, are buried with Christ, and are

resurrected unto new life in Christ, we are now able to drink into one Spirit. **Now the Spirit of God becomes our teacher** and our gentle guide who will lead us to as much Truth as we will receive (see **John 16:13**). However, He will not force you to obey; He will guide you to obey, and it is up to you to obey or not to obey the Word of God He teaches. He will do this through ministry and gifts in the Body of Christ, such as Apostles, Bishops, Prophets, Evangelists, Pastors, Teachers, and other brothers and sisters in the Body of Christ (**Ephesians 4:11-16**). He will also do it as you have communion with Him daily through meditation on His Word, living a life of prayer and worship, and setting aside a time to be intimate with Him (**1John 2:20, 1John 2:27, 1Corinthians 2:9-16, and Galatians 1:16**).

As you listen and follow the model that **the Spirit of God reveals through the life of Jesus Christ on earth**, He will teach you how to move into victory over the devil. You will need to receive the empowerment of the Spirit of God to correctly strike the enemy with the Sword of the Lord, which is the Word of God. Notice that Jesus Christ was baptized because it symbolized His death, burial, and resurrection, which it was! Then, when He came out of the baptismal water, the Heavens opened, a light shone upon him, and the voice of God spoke, and the Holy Spirit as a dove came upon Him to lead Him to the desert.

If Jesus needed the Holy Spirit to begin His ministry on earth and accomplish what God placed Him in the world to do, what makes you think you do not need the Holy Spirit and His Power to fulfill the real purpose God put you here on earth to accomplish? Whether it is to minister or to dominate the business world, you will not be able to accomplish it without the person of the Holy Spirit upon you to defeat the enemy in the desert. Many are going into the desert and ignoring the Holy Spirit; therefore, they are defeated and cannot come out of the desert with the Power to bless others and fulfill the divine destiny God has placed for them.

It is only by obeying Jesus Christ and receiving the Holy Spirit as our teacher and guide, and the Power of God to manifest the Kingdom of God, that we will effectively bear witness to others. The Father promised that the Holy Ghost and Fire would come upon those who believed and that Jesus Christ was the One who administers the Holy Ghost and Fire's baptism with the evidence of speaking in tongues, prophesying, and much more. Read these scriptures regarding the same: (**Matthew 3:11; Mark 16:15-20; I Corinthians 1:12-14; 4:6;14:18 and Acts 1:4-5; 8; 2:1-21; 8:4-18; 9:17-20; 10:44- 46; 18:24-28; 19:1-7**).

We must understand that we are now one with God by Grace in Christ Jesus **(see I Corinthians 6:17;19; I John 4:17-18 and John 14:10-29; 15:4-7)**. Many in the Body of Christ who have confessed Jesus as Lord and Savior are indifferent, full of religious acts and rituals that have led them to become stale; when this happens, the gossip, murmuring, and all manner of carnality begin to manifest. This behavior occurs because they have not been taught right or have chosen not to accept the Truth of God's Word. They get stuck and will not move forward until they take the Truth of God's Word as the Absolute Truth and do what the Word says, regardless of any other source of information, experience, or self-opinion.

Many have failed to realize that Jesus Christ, because He was conceived in the womb of Mary, is the example of every baby of God, child of God, son, or daughter of God. **Luke 1:35** speaks of Jesus being born of the Spirit, and without this, He would not have been alive unto God as the second and final Adam (Man). He is then taken and grows as a child, having every need met yet facing attempts against His life. He was a child, and death was after Him because He was alive. Nevertheless, God preserved His child as He preserves us.

We see in **John 16:13** that Jesus only gained this understanding because He was drinking from the Spirit, who was His teacher and guide. He only spoke and understood as the Holy Spirit guided Him. In the same manner, every born-again believer has access to drink into one Spirit. The Word of God declares:

> **For by one Spirit are we all baptized into one body**, whether we be Jews or Gentiles, whether we be bond or free; and **have been all made to drink into one Spirit. (I Corinthians 12:13)**

During this process, Jesus, who had a soul, mind, will, and emotions just like us, had to forsake the thoughts and temptations of His fleshly body as He walked on earth. His natural body was subject to death because of the first man's sin, and only by the teaching and power of the Holy Spirit was He able to overcome carnal, sinful desires. **Now, we drink into the same Spirit and are ONE SPIRIT with the Lord**, who has been given the power to do the same.

I Corinthians 6:17
"But He that is joined unto the Lord is ONE SPIRIT."

We have been given the Grace and gift of righteousness to rule and reign in this life by Jesus Christ that as He is in Heaven, so are we on the earth (see **Romans 5:17 and I John 4:17**). We are to rule on this earth! We are to demonstrate the Kingdom of God through the leading of the Spirit of God in us, unleashing His power to leave a lasting impact (see **Luke 17:21**).

As we mentioned earlier, Jesus is not sick, lacking, or impoverished. Jesus is not depressed, defeated, in want, or confused. He is not frustrated or worried, and as our perfect example, we are to be just like Him on earth as He is in Heaven if we truly believe His Word. Jesus, being the King of kings and Lord of lords, by His decree, has promoted each person who believes in HIM to be a joint heir with Him (see **Romans 8:14-17**). As mentioned previously, each one of us has a throne, a crown, and a ring of authority so that we can bring forth His will into this earth, in Y'shua-Jesus' name, amen.

God has elevated us who are in Christ into His image (see **Romans 8:29**), and He expects us to bring forth His will on earth. He expects us to do it because we are the sons and daughters of God, the ones who bring God, who is Spirit, into the sight of men and women who depend solely on the visible material world. Through us, the Church, His body, the Body of Christ on earth, God shows His Love, His Faith, and His Hope to bless those who are on the planet and even those in space who have not received Jesus as their Lord and Savior, that by obeying God and sharing the Good News they might be saved in Jesus name, amen.

Exodus 7:1
"And the LORD said unto Moses, See, I have made thee a god to Pharaoh: and Aaron thy brother shall be thy prophet."

I recall the time I heard a man of God teaching on the verse above, which led me to the revelation by the Holy Spirit that when God is in us and we obey Him, He makes us a god to this world and every ungodly circumstance surrounding us. All to bring God's will to the world and fix what the devil attempts to destroy. We must be conscious that this is not because of ourselves but because God lives in us (see **Galatians 2:20**).

Jesus' Kingdom is that of kings and priests, which He has made us. The lowest form of a kingdom is that of slaves! But when you have a Kingdom of kings and priests, now you are talking of it being governed by the Greatest King of all, God. It takes only abuse and mistreatment to have slaves. But it takes another type of King to develop kings and kingdoms, which willfully submit to Him without force but, instead, because of love and knowing that the Ultimate King has our best interest at heart, we obey Him (see **Revelation 17:14**).

Now, as Jesus Christ completed His mission on earth, we are to do the same. To accomplish this, we must operate out of the mind and mindset that is now our own, which is of Christ. Remember, as we mentioned in chapter four, "Restoring the Mind and Mindset of Christ as our own."

I Corinthians 2:16
"For who hath known the mind of the Lord, that he may instruct him? But we have the mind of Christ."

According to **I Corinthians 2:10-14**, because we have received the Spirit of God as our own and as we do what He instructs us through His Word and Life, we can speak and establish, as manifested sons and daughters of God, the will of God on earth, as it is in Heaven, in Jesus name, amen.

> Let this mind be in you, which was also in Christ Jesus: Who, being in the form of God, thought it not robbery to be equal with God: But made himself of no reputation, and took upon Him the form of a servant, and was made in the likeness of men. And being found in fashion as a man, he humbled himself, and became obedient unto death, even the death of the cross. Wherefore God also hath highly exalted him, and given him a name which is above every name: (**Philippians 2:5-9**)

You must allow the Word of God, which the Spirit of God brings to your mind by reading the Bible, to become your own and realize that as you live in the Spirit and speak, your words are eternal, for they are no longer your own. Because you are born of the Spirit, it has now become your mind, the Mind of Christ, the Mind of God, the Mind of the Spirit. **John 14:10** shows us precisely that the Father is in the Son and the Son in the Father. **Jesus did not speak out of His own opinion or soul but rather forsook it so that only the Will of the Father was manifested.** Now the good news is we can, too, by the Spirit of God in us, yield to the Father, and He will do in us for His good pleasure as it is written in **Philippians 2:13** *"For it is God which worketh in you both to will and to do of his good pleasure."*

Further, the Word of God declares;

> A good man out of the good treasure of his heart bringeth forth that which is good, and an evil man out of the evil treasure of his heart bringeth forth that which is evil: for of the abundance of the heart (MIND) his mouth speaketh. (**Luke 6:45**)

Our job is ONLY to BELIEVE! Repeatedly, we are told not to fear (**John 6:28-29 and Mark 5:36**), saying, "**Be not afraid, only believe.**" This is what Jesus speaks to us through His eternal voice. *If you can believe me (Jesus), I can manifest My Kingdom through you.* Praise God.

Now we have to do away with the Old Mind, that which the devil had put in our minds and initiated a mindset of worry, fear, doubt, double-mindedness, wickedness, lust, jealousy, hate, frustration, and that of a coward. We must now be of Christ Jesus' mindset; as we have His mind, we must also have His mindset. We are of God; we have been made a god to this unbelieving world, that in the name of Jesus Christ, all will know we belong to the Almighty El Elyon, the Most High God, and that Jesus Christ Lives and manifest Himself through each member of His Body, which is who you and I are; the Church of God (**Ephesians 5:30**). HalleluYah! Now we are as BOLD AS LIONS!

Proverbs 28:1
"The wicked flee when no man pursueth; but the righteous are as bold as a lion."

Let me ask you some questions. **Do you approach the things in this life with the ideas and attitude that Jesus approached them, or do you do it with the wicked**

mindset that flees when no one is pursuing them? Also, are you allowing the Devil to deceive you into operating out of a carnal mind, which is the reason why you are being defeated? **Or are you fighting the only fight you are called to fight, which is the fight of faith and defeating the enemy with the Sword of the Spirit, the Word of God?**

I have observed that many people who experience defeat, despair, want, and depression are there because their mindset concerning the circumstances and trials in this life only focuses on earthly things occurring in this visible world. If they would renew their mind and walk in agreement with the Word of God (see **Amos 3:3**) and put in mind, as Mary did, when the angel Gabriel declared that she is highly favored and she answered, "be it unto me" as thou has spoken God, (**Luke 1:38**). They would know, as **Romans 8:37** says, that we are more than conquerors in Christ, and in **II Corinthians 2:14** that God causes us always to triumph in Christ. God has sworn He is not angry with us but, instead, has established His kindness and mercy never to depart from us (see **Isaiah 54:8-10 and Hebrews 8:10-12**). Meaning that if God is for us, nothing can stop us. Praise God (see **Romans 8:31-32 and Joshua 1:5**).

Respond with the Mindset of Christ

People of God, let us respond with the mindset of Christ, as Jesus did. Now is your time, people of God, to move forward in faith and do what the Spirit of God in you desires, which is to manifest the Glory of our Lord Jesus Christ through each one of us by demonstrating the Kingdom of God. By the power of the Holy Ghost and the power of His Fire, we must be utterly intoxicated with the Spirit and not drunk from the wine of the world. This means that we do not receive anything the world offers us to rob us of living an honorable life that God alone has for us.

It is time to abide under the influence of the Holy Ghost and Fire in Jesus' Name, amen. **Ephesians 5:18** states, *"And be not drunk with wine, wherein is excess; but be filled with the Spirit."* We should be so intoxicated with the Spirit that we will do the impossible, and it will not make any sense in the natural world. Take a look at the following scriptures.

> Others mocking said, These men are full of new wine. But Peter, standing up with the eleven, lifted up his voice, and said unto them, Ye men of Judaea, and all ye that dwell at Jerusalem, be this known unto you, and hearken to my words: For these are not drunken, as ye suppose, seeing it is but the third hour of the day. 16 But this is that which was spoken by the prophet Joel; (**Acts 2:13-16 KJV**)

Up to the age of thirty, the Holy Spirit led Jesus; however, the Holy Spirit came upon Him with power, as He was to engage and serve others in ministry. Before the manifestation of His assignment, the Holy Ghost came upon Him to manifest the power of the Kingdom of God. When Jesus was baptized, the Heavens opened, a voice spoke from Heaven, and the Holy Spirit came upon Him as a Dove and led Him to the desert. Had Jesus gone into the desert without the Holy Ghost empowering Him and leading Him, He could not have overcome the enemy and returned in the full demonstration of the Kingdom of God with signs and wonders following everywhere He went.

Since Jesus, the apostles, and the hundred and twenty followers of Jesus in the upper room in Jerusalem are our examples in that they needed the Holy Ghost and Fire to fulfill their ministry, you and I are no exception. Listen, John baptized Jesus in water, but Jesus baptizes all who believe in Him in the Holy Ghost and Fire. **Matthew 3:11** says: *"I indeed baptize you with water unto repentance.* **but he that cometh after me (Jesus) is mightier than I, whose shoes I am not**

***worthy to bear: he shall baptize you with the Holy Ghost,
and with fire:"***

The following scriptures prove that this promise is for
every believer willing to step in faith into the Spiritual lake of
the Holy Ghost and Fire. This lake is where they crucify their
fleshly desires and allow Jesus, who waits to submerge them
in power and fire, to serve others by demonstrating the
Kingdom of God in His name.

> And, being assembled together with them,
> commanded them that they should not depart from
> Jerusalem, but wait for the promise of the Father,
> which, saith he, ye have heard of me. 5 <u>For John truly
> baptized with water</u>; **but ye shall be baptized with
> the Holy Ghost not many days hence**. (Acts 1:4-5)

Notice the words "***ye shall***," which means you shall, or that it
will absolutely come to be that you who believe will have the
same experience of being submerged in the Holy Ghost and
Fire. HalleluYah! **Take it by faith now!**

> But ye shall receive power, after that the Holy Ghost is
> come upon you: and ye shall be witnesses unto me
> both in Jerusalem, and in all Judaea, and in Samaria,
> and unto the uttermost part of the earth. (**Acts 1:8**)

Now, this happens to every believer suddenly. This means
at any time, in any place, all of a sudden, if you believe the
Holy Spirit is willing to come upon you with power so that
you may serve the Lord your God with authority in Jesus'
name to all those around you.

> And when the day of Pentecost was fully come, they
> were all with one accord in one place. (2) **And
> suddenly there came a sound from heaven as of a
> rushing mighty wind, and it filled all the house
> where they were sitting. (3) And there appeared**

unto them cloven tongues like as of fire, and it sat upon each of them. (4) **And they were all filled with the Holy Ghost, and began to speak with other tongues, as the Spirit gave them utterance.** (5) And there were dwelling at Jerusalem Jews, devout men, out of every nation under heaven. (6) Now when this was noised abroad, the multitude came together, and were confounded, because that every man heard them speak in his own language. (7) And they were all amazed and marveled, saying one to another, Behold, are not all these which speak Galilaeans? (8) And how hear we every man in our own tongue, wherein we were born? (9) Parthians, and Medes, and Elamites, and the dwellers in Mesopotamia, and in Judaea, and Cappadocia, in Pontus, and Asia, (10) Phrygia, and Pamphylia, in Egypt, and in the parts of Libya about Cyrene, and strangers of Rome, Jews and proselytes, (11) Cretes and Arabians, we do hear them speak in our tongues the wonderful works of God. (12) And they were all amazed, and were in doubt, saying one to another, What meaneth this? (13) Others mocking said, These men are full of new wine. (14) But Peter, standing up with the eleven, lifted up his voice, and said unto them, Ye men of Judaea, and all ye that dwell at Jerusalem, be this known unto you, and hearken to my words: (15) For these are not drunken, as ye suppose, seeing it is but the third hour of the day. (16) But this is that which was spoken by the prophet Joel; (17) **And it shall come to pass in the last days, saith God, I will pour out of my Spirit upon all flesh:** and your sons and your daughters shall prophesy, and your young men shall see visions, and your old men shall dream dreams: (18) And on my servants and on my handmaidens **I will pour out in those days of my Spirit;** and they shall prophesy: (19) And I will shew wonders in heaven above, and signs in the earth beneath; blood, and fire, and vapour of smoke: (20) The sun shall be turned into darkness, and the moon into blood, before the great and notable day of the Lord come: (21) And it shall come to pass, that whosoever shall call on the name of the Lord shall be saved. (**Acts 2:2-21 KJV**)

Another illustration;

While Peter yet spake these words, **the Holy Ghost fell on all them which heard the word.** And they of the circumcision which believed were astonished, as many as came with Peter, because that on the Gentiles also was poured out the gift of the Holy Ghost. **For they heard them speak with tongues, and magnify God.** (Acts 10:44-46)

It happened again with the Apostle Paul, who came across some believers who had only received the message that John the Baptist preached to them and had not yet received or been empowered by the Holy Ghost. It says that as they were walking, suddenly they encountered the Apostle Paul, led by the Holy Spirit, and because they believed, they also received this experience.

And it came to pass, that, while Apollos was at Corinth, Paul having passed through the upper coasts came to Ephesus: and finding certain disciples, He said unto them, **Have ye received the Holy Ghost since ye believed? And they said unto him, We have not so much as heard whether there be any Holy Ghost.** And he said unto them, Unto what then were ye baptized? And they said, Unto John's baptism. Then said Paul, John verily baptized with the baptism of repentance, saying unto the people, that they should believe on him which should come after him, that is, on Christ Jesus. When they heard this, they were baptized in the name of the Lord Jesus. And when Paul had laid his hands upon them, the Holy

Ghost came on them; and they spake with tongues, and prophesied. And all the men were about twelve. (**Acts 19:1-7**)

All of this reveals that every believer needs the Holy Spirit to come upon them to fulfill their mission here on earth with power and effectiveness. You can find yourself a believer who understands that Jesus Christ is the Messiah and that you are saved, but, **like Apollos, you can be limited in eloquence and might in understanding the scriptures. Still, God desires to take you to another level if you humble yourself before Him and accept His Word.**

And a certain Jew named **Apollos**, born at Alexandria, an **eloquent man and mighty in the scriptures**, came to Ephesus. 25 This man was instructed in the way of the Lord; and **being fervent in the spirit, he spake and taught diligently the things of the Lord, knowing only the baptism of John.** 26 And he began to speak boldly in the synagogue: whom <u>when Aquila and Priscilla had heard, they took him unto them, and expounded unto him the way of God more perfectly.</u> 27 And when he was disposed to pass into Achaia, the brethren wrote, exhorting the disciples to receive him: who, when he was come, helped them much which had believed through grace: 28 For he mightily convinced the Jews, and that publicly, showing by the scriptures that Jesus was Christ. (**Acts 18:24-28**)

It is time to put aside all human-made doctrines. Saints, it is time to understand that your denomination will not save you. Your religion will not save you. Only Jesus Christ, who died on the Cross, saves a person who repents of their sin. By Him and in Him, we are called to be one, standing in unity and boldly declaring what the Word of God teaches. It is written in **I Corinthians 1:12-14**, *"Now this I say, that every one of you saith, I am of Paul; and I of Apollos; and I of Cephas; and I of Christ. Is Christ divided? Was Paul crucified for you?*

Or were ye baptized in the name of Paul? I thank God that I baptized none of you, but Crispus and Gaius." They fought among each other because they were carnal believers. They chose a teacher to instruct them in the doctrines of Christ, and they were carnally opposed to each other, even though they were being taught the same doctrines. Neither Paul, Apollos, nor Cephas taught their own doctrines. They all taught that Christ Jesus is Lord. Stick with the Word's teachings and forsake anything that is not according to the Word of God so that we may all speak as one in Jesus' name, amen.

You see, it goes beyond our interpretation of the Word of God. Only the Holy Spirit and power can bring about a clear understanding of the Word of God. As believers, we must have the same mind, spirit, and action as Jesus Christ because we follow Him. The natural reasoning of men and the human-made religious opinions of God have hindered the church's growth for too long and have caused many brothers and sisters to be put against each other. It is time to return to the Holy Spirit of God and His Word of power alone. Let go of the eloquence of speech and the enticing words of man's wisdom as written:

> And my speech and my preaching was not with enticing words of man's wisdom, but in demonstration of the Spirit and of power:
> **(I Corinthians 2:4)**
> And these things, brethren, I have in a figure transferred to myself and to Apollos for your sakes; that ye might learn in us not to think of men above that which is written, that no one of you be puffed up for one against another. **(I Corinthians 4:6)**

Body of Christ, the only thing the devil will respect is the power of God in your life and the revelation of whom and what God has made you for His Glory. Phillip understood this and won the entire city of Samaria for the Lord, for he was full of the Holy Spirit of God. Yet though God used him to save them and baptize them in water, He used Peter and John to lay hands on them to fill them with the Holy Spirit and power. Why? Because we are all to edify one another in love with the gift God has made us to one another.

Therefore they that were scattered abroad went everywhere preaching the word. 5 **Then Philip went down to the city of Samaria, and preached Christ unto them. 6 And the people with one accord gave heed unto those things which Philip spake, hearing and seeing the miracles which he did.** 7 For unclean spirits, crying with loud voice, came out of many that were possessed with them: and many taken with palsies, and that were lame, were healed. 8 And there was great joy in that city. 9 But there was a certain man, called Simon, which beforetime in the same city used sorcery, and bewitched the people of Samaria, giving out that himself was some great one: 10 To whom they all gave heed, from the least to the greatest, saying, This man is the great power of God. 11 And to him they had regard, because that of long time he had bewitched them with sorceries. 12 But when they believed Philip preaching the things concerning the kingdom of God, and the name of Jesus Christ they were baptized, both men and women. 13 Then Simon himself believed also: and when he was baptized, he continued with Philip, and wondered, beholding the miracles and signs which were done. 14 Now when the apostles which were at Jerusalem heard that Samaria had received the word of God, **they sent unto them Peter and John:** 15 Who, when they were come down, prayed for them, that they might receive the Holy Ghost: 16 (For as yet he was fallen upon none of them: only they were baptized in the name of the Lord Jesus.) 17 Then laid they their hands on them, and they received the Holy Ghost. 18 And when Simon saw that through laying on of the apostles' hands the Holy Ghost was given, he offered them money. (**Acts 8:4-18**)

Commissioned to preach with power, the Word of God describes Jesus Christ commissioning us, His Church, to preach the Good News of the Gospel to every creature and that signs and wonders will follow them that believe.

> And he said unto them, **Go ye into all the world, and preach the Gospel to every creature.** He that believeth and is baptized shall be saved; but he that believeth not shall be damned. And **these signs shall follow them that believe; In my name shall they cast out devils; they shall speak with new tongues; They shall take up serpents; and if they drink any deadly thing, it shall not hurt them; they shall lay hands on the sick, and they shall recover.** So then after the Lord had spoken unto them, he was received up into heaven, and sat on the right hand of God. <u>And they went forth, and preached everywhere, the Lord working with them, and confirming the word with signs following. Amen.</u> (**Mark 16:15-20**)

Notice that the apostles preached the Word, and the Word was confirmed with miracles, signs, and wonders. One might say, but they are the apostles, that is why, but notice the scriptures and that Jesus said this is for all who believe, not just the apostles, but for all believers, including you who believe. Let us look at Ananias, a disciple and follower of Jesus, who believed this promise and was used by God to lay hands on Saul, also known as the Apostle Paul.

> And **Ananias** went his way, and entered into the house; **and putting his hands on him said**, Brother Saul, the Lord, even Jesus, that appeared unto thee in the way as thou camest, hath sent me, **that thou mightest receive thy sight, and be filled with the Holy Ghost. And immediately there fell from his**

eyes as it had been scales: and he received sight forthwith, and arose, and was baptized. And when he had received meat, he was strengthened. Then was Saul certain days with the disciples which were at Damascus. **And straightway he preached Christ in the synagogues, that he is the Son of God.** (Acts 9:17-20)

The Apostle Paul shows us that once you are filled with the Holy Spirit, you cannot help but preach and proclaim that Jesus Christ is the Son of God.

Furthermore, the Apostle Paul teaches us how the gift of tongues should be used and how He also spoke in tongues. In **I Corinthians 14:18** it states that he said, *"I thank my God, I speak with tongues more than ye all."* All of this teaches the believer that we are, as believers, to be baptized in water. Also, the believers are to be filled and baptized in the Holy Spirit to have the power to serve others with faith in God, to demonstrate the Kingdom of God in Jesus' name. All of this must take place in believers' lives to reveal to the world God whom they cannot see, that they might turn to God and believe.

Does this mean I won't ever make Mistakes?

It would be amazing if, after being born again of God's Spirit and baptized in the Holy Spirit with evidence of speaking in tongues, we would never make mistakes again. However, I am here to tell you that mistakes will be made along the way. But the good news is that despite our mistakes, the Holy Spirit will honor the blood of Jesus Christ that was shed on the cross of Calvary and continue to teach you and lead you as you turn to Him and learn from the mistakes made. God is well aware of the unregenerate bodies our spirits abide in and that our souls are in the process of regeneration as we renew our minds to His Living Word. So when a mistake is made, come to Him, ask for forgiveness, and move forward under the power of the blood of the Lamb of God, who has remitted our sins and made provision for our growth despite our mistakes along our journey in maturing as His sons and daughters.

I recall the many times I have made mistakes along the way, and to this day, I might not fully be aware of the mistakes I am making. Nevertheless, the times I have felt as if the mistakes I made were just too many for God to continue to use me, the Holy Spirit led me to this confession, which by faith I know is my portion, and I hope you make it your own as He leads you to. I now say, **"Despite my mistakes, watch God bless me like you have not seen or heard of anyone being blessed before in their lives."** Thank you, **Y'shua-Jesus Messiah, for, by your merits and grace,** I can behold your majestic Glory as one of your sons in victory. Amen!

"Restoring Mankind's True Identity"

CHAPTER SIX

Speaking as the Oracles of God

Speaking as the Oracles of God

> If any man speak, **let him speak as the oracles of God**; if any man minister, let him do it as of the ability which God giveth: that God in all things may be glorified through Jesus Christ, to whom be praise and dominion for ever and ever. Amen. **(I Peter 4:11)**

What we decide to meditate on and think about will lead us to speak and go in that direction. So whether we speak words of life or lazy, useless, barren words, it will cause a harvest of that sort. We decide the words that will come out of our mouths. So now I have to ask, "**What have you been speaking lately?**" Are you speaking the words of life and blessing that will lead you to make earth as it is in Heaven? Or have you been speaking the words of carnality, inspired by the world, bringing about death and producing no life?

You see, everything you have now, or ever will have, is directly tied to the steering wheel of your tongue. Your tongue will cause you to speak your path in a specific direction that will produce the results you will have. That is why, at this point in this book, it is essential to have discovered that we now have the mind of Christ and are one with Him, that we speak and create what God's Word has instructed us to speak, because He made us operate that way. Many times, you hear it said, "**Speak your mind,**" but really, **the only thing they have been doing is speaking the devil's mind,** for they listen to their flesh, which is corrupt, and the source of all corruption is the devil.

> A man's belly shall be satisfied with the fruit of his mouth; and with the increase of his lips shall he be filled. Death and life are in the power of the tongue: and they that love it shall eat the fruit thereof. **(Proverbs 18:20-21)**

God shows us in His Word that we are responsible for what we receive on this earth. He has given us a choice to satisfy our bellies with what we speak. He has given us the power of life or death Think about this. The words we speak can give life or bring death. They can cause division and strife or cause joy and gladness.

God has made it so that man shall have whatsoever they speak and create. The fact of the matter is that men without God are the way they are because they have chosen to speak death and separation from God. They continue to be deceived by Satan into speaking the evil, which, though it may cause them to gain the world, they lose their soul in the process and end up with an empty life void of any absolute joy. They have been separated from their one true love, who is God. He alone can fulfill the joy of all individuals through Jesus Christ our Lord.

Jesus teaches us that our words show what is in us, according to **Matthew 12:33-36 and Matthew 12:37**. Here, it says that *by the words we speak*, we will either be justified and therefore **produce life**, or by the words we speak, we will be condemned and **produce death**. It is no longer a matter of saying what is on our minds, for humanity was never designed to operate without God. Man and woman were initially created living souls, made in the image and likeness of God and designed to speak out of the source of their Creator, who is Spirit and life, to bring life into this world.

However, because Satan deceived the woman and man, Satan, through what became fallen humanity, began to produce upon this earth the results of his voice to which humanity decides to listen, which is evil and perverse. Therefore, confusion has set in the human race, from not understanding **evolution** and believing that a type of ape gave birth to a human, which at best adds up to an educated guess that equals an opinion. Evolution in its pure form is good and takes humanity made in the image and likeness of God from glory to glory by the Holy Spirit. **However, evolution to fallen humanity only mutates from sin to more sin that takes multi-forms of distortions and corruptions, void of God.** Fallen humanity fails to comprehend that God can do anything, even change a human into the form of an animal as He did with King Nebuchadnezzar, taking him from king to being made as an animal and then restoring Nebuchadnezzar to being king in **Daniel 4:25-35**, showing forth that God is Omnipotent and Omniscient. Now, all humanity has a choice at this very moment to speak words that are of God, that will bring restoration and victory to anything they will face in this life. Or they can continue to speak words of doubt, evil, and misfortune, and continue to reap the results of destruction and death that they have been experiencing.

The good news is that Jesus Christ came not only to make us aware of this but to restore to us the ability to speak and create with the very words of God our Father. In **James 3:3-4**, the Word of God teaches us that our tongue is the steering wheel of our lives and that we decide what direction to navigate in life, be it that of a blessed life full of God or that of a cursed life full of Satan.

It goes on to teach us in **James 3:10-13** that we cannot continue to bless and curse out of what we speak. The illustration given is that of a fountain that gives out sweet and bitter water simultaneously, which is not possible. We cannot continue to allow the "**old man's mindset**" (**that which is of sin**) to speak out of the mouth, which has been made new through the life of the Spirit of God because of Jesus. We must not allow any corrupt communication to proceed out of our mouth but only that which will edify and cause grace to come to the hearer (see **Ephesians 4:29-31**).

In us, through Jesus Christ, God's Spirit has given us the power to tame the tongue that men without God cannot do.

We must now put away all evil speech of depravity, trouble, naughtiness, and wickedness inspired by Satan that leads to death. In **II Timothy 3:8**, it shows that corrupt speaking implies corrupt minds of the old fallen man that was an enemy of God and is an enemy of faith, in which we who are born again of God's life are to have no participation. **Proverbs 23:7** declares, "*As a man thinketh in his heart so is he...*" and now, as you think, you will speak. Therefore, **speak positively of all of God's goodness and blessings.** Speak faith and remember that Jesus said in **Mark 11:23** that you would have what you say, so **do not allow your own words to work against you**. Remember, we are to be imitators of God and, therefore, speak those things that be not as though they were (see **Ephesians 5:1 and Romans 4:17**).

It is essential to know that the One who will carry out the message given to the messenger is the One who gave it to be delivered. In other words, the messenger only delivers the message he was told to give by the one who will make that message good and demonstrate its fullness. This statement is essential to understand. It is God who has called us, and it is He who has equipped us and will make good what He has commanded us to proclaim and communicate throughout the whole earth. Jesus said that when we go and proclaim the Gospel of the Kingdom of God in His name, if the people do not accept it, they who did not receive it would not be rejecting the messengers but rather He who gave them the message to proclaim.

As God has called you and me to **speak as His oracles (utterances)** we must do it knowing we have become one with His Word. When we choose to speak the Word of God, it is God speaking, and we are now one. It has to get to the point that when we speak, we know God is speaking by the Grace given to us by Jesus Christ, our Lord, in whom we abide. So that, as we are speaking, we are not speaking, but He is speaking through us, His channel upon the earth.

We must arise in boldness to declare His Word and to serve others with the Gospel, to know that He, who gave us the message and His precious promises, is the one responsible for manifesting it and making it good to those who have received His mercy and Grace. The days of being timid and ashamed are over for every member of the Body of Christ Jesus, as He has come upon us with His Holy Spirit. He gives us the power of His Word to make it known that the Kingdom of God has come near to all those to whom His Word is proclaimed.

Without a doubt, it is vital that we understand the value of the words and messages we decide to give to others. As the members of the Body of Christ, you and I are responsible for only saying what He instructs us to say. Nothing more, nothing less. If we do this, not only will we live in total victory, but others will see the Glory of the Lord through our lives. For we are living testimonies of God's faithfulness, as He is watching over every word He has spoken to us to perform it, as it is written in **Jeremiah 1:12**.

Off With His Head

The King of kings has declared OFF WITH HIS HEAD! Remember the first principle, "**We must believe the WORD of GOD.**" It does not matter how much you pray or fast or how many times you go to church; if you do not believe the Word of God, you will not receive His promises. In **II Peter 1:2,** it states, *"Grace and peace be multiplied unto you through the knowledge of God, and of Jesus our Lord."* **God does not lie** (see **Hebrews 6:18, Titus 1:2, and Romans 3:4**). No matter what you face in the natural world with your husband, wife, finances, children, sickness, business, job, or anything else. These issues do not stand a chance if you believe God's Word!

I came to tell you and reaffirm that what Jesus did on the Cross has granted us the Kingdom of God, and GRACE has made us His Righteousness [see **II Corinthians 5:21 and James 5:16**), which talks about the prayer of a Righteous man is now our prayers. You are FREE, DELIVERED, HEALED, BLESSED, LOVED, ACCEPTED BY GOD BY GRACE, AND YOU HAVE THE VICTORY OVER THE DEVIL. It does not matter if you are young or old. What matters is your faith in God and the authority God has given you in Chris Jesus, our Lord.

Most of us are facing what we are facing because we do not know our rightful place in the Body of Christ. One of the things God reminded me about is that the devil has been stripped of his power (**Hebrews 2:14**). Jesus Christ has destroyed the works of the devil and has spoiled all the devil's principalities and powers (**Colossians 2:14-15**). Satan has no authority over the believer (**Luke 10:19**), and he has no power over the people who trust and love God, who have entered into a covenant believing in Jesus Christ.

Satan is underneath our feet, and he cannot stop us because God is for us. Although this is the Truth, it is up to us to enforce our rights to go beyond the lying boundaries of Satan because God certainly does not put any restraints on us. God said in **Ephesians 3:20** that He can *"Do exceedingly and abundantly above what you can ask or imagine according to the power that is working in you."* Just because someone else has not been able to do something that seems impossible to accomplish does not mean it will be impossible for you, for with God, all things are possible (**Mark 9:23**).

God has taken the limits off the believers so that humanity can be in awe. When they come to question and ask, "How did you do that?' You can point and say, "It is not me, but God." God's Word says, *"For with men this is impossible, but with God all things are possible"* (**Luke 18:27**). You must know that the devil has no authority in your life. Today, see how God sees you and what He has made you. You can come and stand against anything that is not of God that gets in your way, and you can cut the head off regardless of what it may be (see **Hebrews 2:14; Colossians 2:15 and Revelations 1:18**). The message God has called me to share with you is that the King of kings has declared unto you, His people, "**Off with his head!**"

You have the power to cut the head off anything in the world that seems bigger than you; it may seem that it will take you down or that you cannot overcome it in the natural world, but remember God has made you more than a conqueror (**Romans 8:37**). The world is full of chaos; people around you may be full of evil and wickedness. You may be a young man or woman surrounded by people who are full of darkness, experimenting with drugs, sex, the nightlife, and the instant gratification of the senses. You may be feeling uncomfortable within yourself at school, work, or wherever, not knowing how to go about things. Well, today, I have come to tell you what the Lord declares. God says in His Word, "**You are the salt, you are the light, and you are the authority in the midst of darkness**" (see **Matthew 5:13**).

When you show up, you do not have to feel uncomfortable because you are in authority over darkness. When you stand on the scene, all evil must bow down to you because you are a child of God, and you have the Spirit of the Lord, which raised him from the dead (see **Romans 8:11**). You must know that the Holy Spirit dwells in you, that you have the Kingdom of God and the power of God in your life to overcome anything in this world that would try to overpower you.

You have to overcome fear and take it down. You have to cast down those words that tell you that you are restricted and cannot do anything or go forward. Today, I come to say that the devil is a liar, for he is a defeated foe. Jesus Christ has set you free, and you can do all things in Christ (see **Philippians 4:13**). So, join me and dive into the scriptures today. We must believe God's Word and accept who He has made us by His Grace. It is because of what He did and how

He made us that, now, we stand in this place of authority. It is by what He did that we can now operate and speak like Him on the earth as He is in Heaven (**I John 4:17**). As the people of God, we will literally bring the King's will on earth as it is in Heaven. This reality is not just a theological concept, although some have made it to be that, or men's opinion, but what is written in the Word of God. It is the Truth!

Please take a look at **I Samuel 16:6-7** to ensure we all equally understand what God has spoken. Whether you are old, young, or a child, it does not matter. This portion of the scriptures will affirm you because it is the Truth. Say, **"This is the truth!"** Now, if you continue in it, it will make you free. Scripture tells us Saul made a mess, and now the prophet Samuel is sent to anoint the new king that God would show him. Furthermore, Samuel went to Jesse's house because Saul disobeyed God and could no longer hear God.

The prophet Samuel first looked at Eliab and judged him to be God's chosen because of his appearance, and God had to correct his prophet for looking solely at his outward appearance. Then seven sons of Jesse went before him, and the prophet says it is none of these. And then Jesse, the human father of David, who did not consider David to be qualified for anything except to attend to the sheep, remembered him and called for him.

Let me tell you that your natural mom and dad may not look at you as qualified. Humanity may not look at you as being qualified. People around you may look at you and say, "This guy cannot do that! He is not able or educated; he does not have the intellect or finances to do that." Perhaps some leaders might be saying that, for they are not hearing God's voice. It is not that they never heard God's voice, but just at the moment, they may not be hearing God's voice concerning you. And you cannot get mad at them, although the temptation to do so might be there. You have to know that it is God who promotes you. It is God who chooses and calls you. He does not care what age you are.

God looks on the inside and sees what is in your heart. The prophet Samuel was able to hear God. To every leader in the Body of Jesus Christ, I counsel you that if you have a young man, woman, child, or elder that you do not know anything about, fast and pray so that you may hear God regarding them. Put the human-made doctrine aside, put the denominational rules that are not according to the Word of God aside, and seek God in Spirit and in Truth concerning that individual before you pass judgment on them. Seek God, and press in; remember that part of the responsibility God gave you was to encourage and facilitate the expansion of the Kingdom of God.

Because Samuel was able to hear God, he anointed the right person; otherwise, he would have anointed the wrong person and would have been outside the will of God. If that were the case, the person who was supposed to lead would not be placed in that position and would end up not fulfilling the function of the work required of them with good success. God told Samuel, and I am paraphrasing here, *I do not look at the outward appearance. I look at the inside of the heart of a person.* Jesus reaffirms this with the Pharisees and Sadducees. He tells us in **Mark 23:23-27 and Luke 11:38** that you are concerned about the outward, but God looks at the inside of your heart, and if it is for Him. It does not matter if you have many flaws, and you may have a lot of purging that needs to take place. God will teach you discipline, how to talk right, how to walk right, be gentle, love and be kind, and express His love, authority, and Grace. Once He has called you, the purging begins.

When God said, *"**Anoint him**,"* even if the leadership misses it, God is faithful, and He will not forget you. If He has appointed you and if your heart is for Him, it will surely be. Now, it could be at your job that a promotion is coming your way, but your bosses pass you up. Do not get mad at your boss. It could be that God has something better in mind for you than that. He may want you to own your own business with people under you, or God may be keeping you from having to endure hardship in that new position. This seeming foresight could be an opportunity to reveal your response to being overlooked for a promotion. This circumstance will show if God can promote you.

The Spirit of Truth will guide you, as stated in **John 16:13**. The field has been leveled, and all who trust God have access to Him. Next, Samuel anointed David as king among his brothers, and his brothers did not take it lightly. You can read more about this in the next chapter. Remember, the message of God is, **"Off with his head!"** You must rise up against the things that are of the lustful flesh, like sin and the world influence that Satan would use, and cut off its head.

In keeping with the Word of God, in **I Samuel 17**, the Philistines gathered for battle against Israel and Saul! **I Samuel 17:4-11** shows Saul as afraid because he was listening to this 10-foot-tall man who had heavy armor and was big and intimidating. In the natural world, he was intimidating! What happened to Saul is that he lost his ability to hear God because he did things his way and disobeyed God. Let me tell you today that the reason why you may have the problems you have, whether consciously or ignorantly, is because you may be sowing in the lust of the flesh, and you do not even know it.

Somewhere along the line, you sowed in the lust of the flesh, and now you are in that situation. But let me tell you that God is merciful and declares in **Psalm 50:15**, "*And call upon me in the day of trouble: I will deliver thee, and thou shalt glorify me.*" Saul lost the ability to call upon God and hear Him. All Saul could listen to was the lust of the flesh and the taunting of the giant, which caused him to fear.

My brothers and sisters, what giant is speaking to you

today? What giant is threatening you today? You, who may not know God, if you think there are giants in the land and the natural world, you are right. These giants are way beyond your ability to destroy them. But if you look to God, you can be like David, one whom God called, even though he was a young man. He was bold, courageous, and understood God's covenant.

I want you to stop and meditate on what has come against you. If you are a minister, I want you to ask yourself, **"What is intimidating me?"** Picture the giant against you right now. It could be a pandemic, a layoff at work, a debt beyond your ability to pay, a sickness, or perhaps your home is at risk of being taken away from you, or your children are acting crazy. To this, all you do is focus on the problem and all the negativity. You may say, "There is no way I can do anything here. I feel helpless and defeated! I cannot talk about God here in school or at work." The giants have come to intimidate and restrict you, telling you what you cannot do, but I have come to assure you that God sent His Son, Jesus Christ, so that **by the Sword of the Word of God, you too can rise up against that giant and cut his head off as you are led of God.**

I want you to picture that giant in your mind now and declare unto it today, "This day, I will cut your head off in the name of the Lord Jesus Christ. You will not intimidate me, you will not kill me and feed me to the fowls of the air or the beast of the earth, I will not fall, I will not fail, and I will not die." **Hebrews 2:14**, *"Forasmuch then as the children are partakers of flesh and blood, he also himself likewise took part of the same; that through death he might destroy him that HAD the power of death, that is, the devil;"* **the devil HAD the power of death**—he does not have it anymore!

You must understand this: the devil has no power over you if you have a covenant with God, and you know you also have the angels, the host of Heaven, the anointing, and the

Holy Spirit. The power of God is in your life, and you know you are here in the world to rule over it in Jesus' name. Look at **Colossians 2:15,** which says, *"And having spoiled principalities and powers, he made a shew of them openly, triumphing over them in it."* Jesus spoiled the enemy and all his foes! Jesus Christ has dominion over every kingdom. The devil can only do what you allow him to do by your own words, not by what the devil says; otherwise, you and I would already be dead.

The outcome of what you speak is based on the words you decide to give life to, which is why you must be focused and speak only the Living Word of God. We established that you must cut that giant's head off and any other giant that will try to arise. Let us return to **I Samuel 17:12-26** for an illustration of this. David went out to bring food to his brothers on the battlefield, but when he arrived there, **Goliath came out and spoke,** and I am paraphrasing here, **"Can anyone come and take me on in battle!"** Saul should have been the first one out there, confidently knowing God was with him. However, Saul could not hear God because of his disobedience.

Now David, on the other hand, knowing he had a covenant with God, rose up, not because He was bigger than Saul or Goliath, but because he knew there was a cause and knew God was his strength and his shield. I come to tell you that your reward, harvest, vision, and what God has placed in you is so. If you hear the giant of disunity taunting you and the giant defying the Living God, you are to rise up because you are a man or woman of God. There is a cause, and the reward comes when you cut the giant's head off. But notice you will not kill that giant by focusing on the negative thing that the giant is saying and portraying.

This negativity is what is happening in the world today. Men and women want to do things their way; therefore, rest assured that the world's way will collapse. If they would turn to God, He would give them the wisdom and power to solve the problems the enemy has made for humanity. Instead, they continue to try to solve the problems on their own, driven by greed and the power of the world's systems. Yet, God places us, the believers in Christ Jesus, who want to manifest the blessings and the rewards of God's covenant, to slay the giants of the land.

Listen to David and what he said! "Who is this uncircumcised Philistine?" Out of all the things to say, why did David say this? David talked this way because he understood the covenant God made with Israel. Everything of God was for those included in His covenant, and everything that was not of the covenant must bow down and submit to God or be subdued. What circumstances are you facing outside of the covenant, trying to defy the Living God who has given you a new and better covenant? You must arise in boldness just like David!

In **I Samuel 17:27-29,** it shows that David's brother did not like him having that much courage. But David knew of his covenant with God and, therefore, was unafraid. David trusted in God to do what He said He would do. Knowing that David probably said to himself, "Hey—is there not a cause?" Here lies the reason why He rose up against the giant.

The same now applies to us. Is there not a cause worth fighting for, trusting God in faith for our communities, families, and schools? These causes are why I am here today, and I am as David was: I am after God's own heart and will slay the giant in Jesus' name. In **I Samuel 17:33,** King Saul should have responded like David, but he could not because he could not hear God's voice due to his disobedience. As you read this verse, notice that King Saul tries to discourage David by telling him he cannot defeat the giant because he is too young, and Goliath has been trained to fight from his youth. Saul talked like that because he could not hear from God and only looked at things from a natural worldview. Stop listening to people who cannot hear from God! Love them, help them, but do not listen to them. They are in the flesh and only rely on what is seen in this natural world; they are unaware of the spirit and the unseen world.

Saul told David, "You are a youth, and you cannot fight!" Young people, let me tell you, you can do all things with God, and you can revolutionize your community and everywhere you go if you believe in God. The same goes for every person, regardless of age. David is a great example here because he shows the Truth of God's Word that we *"can do all things through Christ which strengthens us"* (see **Philippians 4:13**). David knew this, but he had to convince King Saul that he could defeat the giant with God as he did with the bear and the lion (see **I Samuel 17:34-37**). David relied solely on God and not on himself to have the giant delivered into his hands.

David had to say, and I am paraphrasing this in my own words, "I know it looks impossible, but God has granted me His anointing with the bear and the lion, and He will grant it to me with this giant, and he will fall," (see **I Samuel 17:37-38**). Afterward, Saul tried putting his armor on David the way he was used to when he prepared for battle, but David took it off because he had not proven it for himself in battle. So David rejected Saul's armor for himself.

What David did has a powerful message for leaders today. Leadership must allow the rising Davids to do it with what God has equipped them and what God has proven in their lives. You cannot take what someone else has done if you have not proven it. Unless you prove it, you cannot use it. God is saying the way I made you is enough to slay the giant.

As it was in **I Samuel 17:40-44** with Israel and David, you must understand the giant is going to speak against you, saying, "I am going to kill you; you will not make it; I will destroy you." He is not going to keep his mouth shut. He will try to intimidate you like he did Saul and all of Israel. Notice

David boldly spoke because he knew of his covenant with God. Now, we have a better covenant through Christ Jesus!

Let us examine the words of David here in **I Samuel 17:45-47** *"Thou comes to me with a sword, and with a spear, and with a shield: but I come to thee in the name of the Lord of hosts, the God of Israel, whom thou hast defied. 46 This day will the Lord deliver thee into mine hand; I will smite thee, and take thine head from thee: and I will give the carcasses of the host of the Philistines this day unto the fowls of the air, and to the wild beasts of the earth; that all the earth may know that there is a God in Israel. 47 And all the assembly shall know that the Lord saveth not with sword and spear: for the battle is the Lord's and he will give you into our hands."* Speak as David spoke and say to the giants of your life—**"this day I will cut your head off!"**

Notice in **I Samuel 17:48** that the giant ran toward him. The giant did not go with his head in shame. After David said what he said, the giant responded, and I am paraphrasing, "Let's see if you can walk the talk." David did not back down; he did not get intimidated but instead ran towards Goliath. You and I must also run toward that giant when he comes against us, and meet him head-on with the stone which is the Word of God! You, just like David, will lay him out in Jesus' name (see **I Samuel 17:49-54**). Praise God!

When you see that giant, take what you have: the Holy Spirit, the name of Jesus, the Blood of Jesus, the Corner Stone, the Rock, the Word of God; you speak it, and it will cause the enemy to fall before your face. No circumstance can defeat you. Believe in the Good News. Cut the giant's head off. You are saved, healed, delivered, blessed, and prosperous. You must rise up boldly knowing your place, which God has empowered you with authority. You are no longer to bow down to the giant. You may look weak, but you are God's vessel through which you will slay the giant and cut off his head by believing you have a covenant with God.

You have read and heard the Truth. If you continue in the Truth, it will make you free. You can win your community, your loved ones, and your school; you can and will slay the giants, be it debt, fear, a pandemic, or anything else. Believe the Good News and know what you have is enough through Christ Jesus. You are the anointed of God. Rise and destroy the works of the devil. You may be up against giants, facing things beyond what you can handle. But let me tell you, Jesus Christ has already defeated the giants for you. Still, He cannot bless you with this victory and teach you how to do this without you receiving the gift of God, Jesus Christ, as your Lord and Savior, and the regenerating power of the Holy Ghost.

It Is Your Time—Only Believe And Fear Not

Our Identity as born-again believers in Christ is with Jesus, and now we are to work the works of God. This would be impossible if we had to do it with our own strength and our own ability, but the good news is that our part is to believe that Jesus has done it and will continue to do it.

> Then said they unto him, What shall we do, that we might work the works of God? Jesus answered and said unto them, This is the work of God, **that ye believe on him whom he hath sent. (John 6:28-29)** As soon as Jesus heard the word that was spoken, he saith unto the ruler of the synagogue, **Be not afraid, only believe. (Mark 5:36)** But when Jesus heard it, he answered him, saying, **Fear not: believe only**, and she shall be made whole. **(Luke 8:50)**

This is all Jesus requires of us and continues to reaffirm: our part is to believe. When something seems beyond you—

ONLY BELIEVE! When they say it cannot be done—**ONLY BELIEVE!** The message God has given me to give to you is, **"IT IS YOUR TIME-ONLY BELIEVE AND FEAR NOT!"** God is for us (see **Romans 8:31**).

God can do nothing for you unless you believe and know **it is your time!** God honors your faith in His Word, rooted in love, but faith without action equals no results. **There is no substitution for action! James 2:17,** "*Even so faith, if it hath not works, is dead, being alone.*" And **James 2:26** "*For as the body without the spirit is dead, so faith without works is dead also.*" I believe God has sent me to the right place, which is your life, to share this amazing news that we are members of the Body of Christ living in the Spirit and being made the visible expression of Him as we do what He says upon the earth.

It is time to rule and reign in Jesus' name! It is time to speak as the Oracles of God. When you speak the Word of God, although it is your voice, it is no different than if God were speaking it if you are His son in Christ Jesus, living in the Spirit of God. Your new positioning in life came only from Jesus' merits and not your own. **After all, what did you do to sin?** In **Romans 5:17**, God's Word tells us, "*For if by one man's offence death reigned by one; much more they which receive abundance of grace and of the gift of righteousness shall reign in life by one, Jesus Christ.*" You were just born into this world, where only one man originally sinned. The same way one man sinned, now through the second and last Adam-Man (Jesus), you are born of the Spirit, now you are the righteousness of God. HalleluYah!

Be born again and overcome the world by faith in Christ Jesus! God's Word declares in **I John 5:4, "*For whatsoever is born of God overcometh the world: and this is the victory that overcometh the world, even our faith.*"** Are you born of God? If you are, then the Word of God here is talking about you and me. The God within us is Almighty! The God in us heals today: saves today, delivers today, prospers today, and blesses today! It is our time! We must **only believe and FEAR NOT!** We can operate like Jesus because of the sacrifice He made on the Cross of Calvary and the New Covenant He established. Praise God!

God's Word declares:

> In a little wrath I hid my face from thee for a moment; but with everlasting kindness will I have mercy on thee, saith the Lord thy Redeemer. For this is as the waters of Noah unto me: for as I have sworn that the waters of Noah should no more go over the earth; **so have I sworn that I would not be wroth with thee, nor rebuke thee.** For the mountains shall depart, and the hills be removed; but my kindness shall not depart from thee, neither shall the covenant of my peace be removed, saith the Lord that hath mercy on thee. **(Isaiah 54:8-10)**

> For this is the covenant that I will make with the house of Israel after those days, saith the Lord; I will put my laws into their mind, and write them in their hearts: and I will be to them a God, and they shall be to me a people: And they shall not teach every man his neighbour, and every man his brother, saying, Know the Lord: for all shall know me, from the least to the greatest. For I will be merciful to their unrighteousness, **and their sins and their iniquities will I remember no more. (Hebrews 8:10-12)**

God has sworn by His own namesake that He is not angry with us. He has justified us through Christ Jesus, and we are now blessed forever and walk in the blessing.

Surely, this is the time to abide under the Influence of the fire of the Holy Ghost in Jesus' Name. To be so intoxicated that you will do the impossible, and it will not make any sense in the natural world. **It is time to abide in the Word of God and live, breathe, and speak in faith.** You will be able to tell what is within by the way that you speak. What is in you? **Romans 1:15** says, *"So, as much as in me is, I am ready to preach the gospel to you that are at Rome also."* It is time to be one with the Word of the Gospel so that you can be ready at all times to share the good news of the Kingdom of God with all people.

It is time to discover the God in you that is always present, always healing, always delivering, always ready to manifest upon all flesh. So it is written in **Colossians 1:27,** *"To whom God would make known what is the riches of the glory of this mystery among the Gentiles; which is Christ in you, the hope of glory:"* It is Christ in us so that we may give life to those around us. We are to be gods to every ungodly situation or circumstance and bring God's will on earth as it is in Heaven. This can only happen as we know who we are as children of God and die to the lust of this world that urges the unregenerate flesh to sin. If you do not believe me, believe the Word of God in the New Testament.

> **But if the Spirit of him that raised up Jesus from the dead dwell in you, he that raised up Christ from the dead shall also quicken your mortal bodies by his Spirit that dwelleth in you.** Therefore, brethren, we are debtors, not to the flesh, to live after the flesh. For if ye live after the flesh, ye shall die: but if ye through the Spirit do mortify the deeds of the body, ye shall live. **For as many as are led by the Spirit of God, they are the sons of God.** For ye have not received the spirit of bondage again to fear; but ye have received the Spirit of adoption, whereby we cry, Abba, Father. The Spirit itself beareth witness with our spirit, that **we are the children of God: And if children, then heirs; heirs of God, and joint-heirs with Christ; if so be that we suffer with him, that we may be also glorified**

together. (Romans 8:11-17)

If you are led by the Spirit, and not the flesh, you are a mature child of God, an heir of God, and joint-heirs with Christ: What He has is what you have by grace through faith. Praise God!

> What shall we then say to these things? If God be for us, who can be against us? He that spared not his own Son, but delivered him up for us all, how shall he not with him also freely give us all things? Who shall lay anything to the charge of God's elect? It is God that justifieth. Who is he that condemneth? It is Christ that died, yea rather, that is risen again, who is even at the right hand of God, who also maketh intercession for us. Who shall separate us from the love of Christ? Shall tribulation, or distress, or persecution, or famine, or nakedness, or peril, or sword? As it is written, For thy sake we are killed all the day long; we are accounted as sheep for the slaughter. **Nay, in all these things we are more than conquerors through him that loved us. (Romans 8:31-37)**

It is time for the manifestation of God's sons (mature believers in Christ) to demonstrate the Kingdom of God to have full proof of faith with works to bless all the families of the earth as the seed of Abraham. God has made us more than conquerors. God told Abram:

> Now the Lord had said unto Abram, Get thee out of thy country, and from thy kindred, and from thy father's house, unto a land that I will shew thee: And I will make of thee a great nation, and I will bless thee, and make thy name great; and thou shalt be a blessing: And I will bless them that bless thee, and curse him that curseth thee: **and in thee shall all families of the earth be blessed. (Genesis 12:1-3)**

Remember that it is time to allow God, who spoke you into existence, to perform you for His Glory as you obey His Word. Stop trying to perform yourself—rebel not against God. He spoke you into existence; He wills and does in you for His good pleasure. Become of no reputation just like Jesus did, as the scriptures show us in **Philippians 2:6-7**. Yield to the Holy Spirit, God who is in you. **Jeremiah 1:12**, *"Then said the Lord unto me, Thou hast well seen: for I will hasten my word to perform it."* God will manifest Himself through you and perform you as you surrender to Him.

Awaken to see with the eyes of faith all that God Almighty is doing in you.

> The eyes of your understanding being enlightened; that ye may know what the hope of his calling is, and what the riches of the glory of his inheritance in the saints. (**Ephesians 1:18**)

Remember, Jesus is our only example, and so are those who imitate Him, but it is He whom we follow!

> And into whatsoever city ye enter, and they receive you, eat such things as are set before you: 9 And heal the sick that are therein, and say unto them, The Kingdom of God is come nigh unto you. (**Luke 10:8-9**)

Our job is to bring the Kingdom of God in us to the people in the world and manifest it by the power of the One who is compassionate with all who will receive Him. Heal the sick, raise the dead, bless and curse not! Minister Grace to the hearer. **I proclaim you blessed! I proclaim you healed and holy!** *Be whole and be prosperous, even as your soul is prosperous!* (3 John 1:2).

You will know you believe if you are at rest and in peace. If you are frustrated, it is not God. If you are in strife, then it is not God. If you are complaining, it is not God. Only believe He will show Himself as you yield and allow Him in and through you to bless the families of the earth as He has made you a blessing. So shout it out loud: **It is time to receive and rest, as I believe and do!**

To accomplish what is mentioned above, you and I must keep our minds on Him.

> For we which have believed do enter into rest, as he said, As I have sworn in my wrath, if they shall enter into my rest: although the works were finished from the foundation of the world. (**Hebrews 4:3**)

> And the peace of God, which passeth all understanding, shall keep your hearts and minds through Christ Jesus. (**Philippians 4:7**)

> Thou wilt keep him in perfect peace, whose mind is stayed on thee: because he trusteth in thee. (**Isaiah 26:3**)

All we have to do is keep His Word, and we will abide in the Blessing. The Word says in **Luke 11:28**, "*But he said, Yea rather, blessed are they that hear the word of God, and keep it.*" We are to do what the Word says about our new and better Covenant. God expects us to allow Him to do the impossible through us on this earth. **Only Believe!**

God calls us to command upon the earth, to do His will on earth as it is in Heaven. For this reason, He created us in His image and gave us His authority. Therefore, the days of not knowing what to do are over for the believer, for the believer believes the Word of God, and what comes forth out of his mouth will be established: **all shall prosper as they believe the prophet (the Living Word of God).**

And they rose early in the morning, and went forth

into the wilderness of Tekoa: and as they went forth, Jehoshaphat stood and said, Hear me, O Judah, and ye inhabitants of Jerusalem; Believe in the Lord your God, so shall ye be established; believe his prophets, so shall ye prosper. **(2 Chronicles 20:20)**

We have also a more sure word of prophecy; whereunto ye do well that ye take heed, as unto a light that shineth in a dark place, until the day dawn, and the day star arise in your hearts: **(2 Peter 1:19)**

As you walk in the light of the Living Almighty God in you, as you speak, it is God speaking if you abide in the Spirit! Therefore, do not rebel against Him so that He can perform through you.

God has made His abode or inhabitation in every believer.

Jesus answered and said unto him, If a man love me, he will keep my words: and my Father will love him, and we will come unto him, and make our abode with him. He that loveth me not keepeth not my sayings: and the word which ye hear is not mine, but the Father's which sent me. These things have I spoken unto you, being yet present with you. But the Comforter, which is the Holy Ghost, whom the Father will send in my name, he shall teach you all things, and bring all things to your remembrance, whatsoever I have said unto you. Peace I leave with you, my peace I give unto you: not as the world giveth, give I unto you. Let not your heart be troubled, neither let it be afraid. **(John 14:23-27)**

You must decide. Will you be one with the fleshly, sinful way of the devil? Or one with the Spirit of Life, which is God? **God said this, not men, not religion.** If you genuinely love God and the people on the earth, you will obey God and be what He has made you, which is a god to every ungodly situation.

You will decree as the King of kings in you, decrees, and it shall be established on earth as it is in Heaven. **Matthew 18:18-19** summarized declares, "**What you bind is bound, what you loosen is loosed.**" **Job 22:28** says, *"Thou shalt also decree a thing, and it shall be established unto thee: and the light shall shine upon thy ways."* As sons and daughters of God, we must speak what the Lord commands in faith, and as we decree it, light shall shine upon our ways.

I am here to tell you that God is releasing you to solve every problem that comes your way by letting Him perform you. **Become of no reputation and allow Him to perform you for His Glory.** You have been set free! Take it, be new, be light, be life! Be love, for it is what He has made you. Receive it! It is time to rely only on God and live by faith rooted in His love. There is no other way to total manifestation for victory but by faith.

You and I are to laugh at anything the enemy would try against us because we believe greater is He in us (**1 John 4:4**) than Satan in the world!

> He shall deliver thee in six troubles: yea, in seven there shall no evil touch thee. In famine he shall redeem thee from death: and in war from the power of the sword. Thou shalt be hid from the scourge of the tongue: neither shalt thou be afraid of destruction when it cometh. At destruction and famine thou shalt laugh: neither shalt thou be afraid of the beasts of the earth. For thou shalt be in league with the stones of the field: and the beasts of the field shall be at peace with thee. And thou shalt know that thy tabernacle shall be in peace; and thou shalt visit thy habitation, and shalt not sin. Thou shalt know also that thy seed shall be great, and thine offspring as the grass of the earth. Thou shalt come to thy grave in a full age, like as a shock of corn cometh in in his season. Lo this, we have searched it, so it is; hear it, and know thou it for

thy good. (**Job 5:19-27**)

He that sitteth in the heavens shall laugh: the Lord shall have them in derision. (**Psalm 2:4 KJV**)

It is time to take action. It is time to do what God says in His word and prove our love to Him daily. Remember, there is no substitution for action. Your actions speak of your faith. Your words speak of your faith. Whether you see it in the natural world or not. It speaks!

It is the time and dispensation of Grace and favor through Jesus our Lord—**ONLY BELIEVE! Psalm 102:13**, *"Thou shalt arise, and have mercy upon Zion: for the time to favour her, yea, the set time, is come."* How is it that grace and favor are going to manifest? **II Peter 1:2**, *"Grace and peace be multiplied unto you through the knowledge of God, and of Jesus our Lord."* By having Faith in the revelation knowledge given to the believer by our teacher, the Holy Spirit through the Word of God, we will see this favor and grace multiplied to us who believe.

Every Direction You Take Forward

How would you like every direction and decision you make to be forward now that you know who you are? Sounds impossible? In the natural world, yes, but you and I know that we serve a supernatural God. By this time, we can come to understand and know that every direction and decision we make is to be in the Spirit. Therefore, every direction taken in the Spirit is forward. Summarizing what Jesus said in **John 3:8**, "the wind blows, but you do not know where it is going or where it came from." Then He compares the life of a Spirit-filled believer to be the same as the wind that blows. Are you ready to take everything you have learned and be led by Him? As you make the vital decision to operate in the Spirit by faith everywhere you go, thinking and speaking like God in Jesus' name will allow God to bring His will to earth through you. **Then, every decision and every direction you go will be forward in the Spirit.** Because of this revelation, we, the believers in Christ Jesus, can live in the God of more than enough, who is El Shaddai. It is essential that we know and grasp all that God has made available to us to walk in total victory. We must stop seeing and observing only the natural earthly things and truly know in the Spirit.

You might be asking yourself, how? Well, the Word of God gives us the knowledge so that we may know and take what we need from God. The Word of God declares:

> *And this is the confidence that we have in him, that, if we ask any thing according to his will, he heareth us: 15 And if we know that he hear us, whatsoever we ask, **we know** that we have the petitions that we desired of him.* (**First John 5:14-15**)

God has allowed us to come into this time of more than enough in Him, where the supernatural lifestyle of His omnipotent love is our lifestyle and nature. A life that gives all that may be needed to those around us and allows us who believe in God to ask anything according to His will, and He grants it. However, we will only receive it from the invisible realm into the visible realm, as **we know** that we have what we desire from Him.

Nevertheless, if you do not know, then you will never see it manifest in your life. As **we know**, it causes us to receive with the net of faith all that He has for us and for others around us. We have been given the privilege to be a blessing to all the families of the earth as the seed of Abraham in Christ Jesus. We literally have treasures in Heaven that are without limits, and they include all heavenly and earthly blessings to live a life that will cause all to behold our God through us and all He does for us.

How is it possible for every direction you go to be forward? The answer is found in **Romans 8:26-27**. When you **know that you know** the perfect will of God by faith in the Word and that the intercession of the Holy Spirit is enough to make every decision you make a forward movement, it is clear to you that you are not doing things by your own strength. You believe and embrace the guidance of the Holy Spirit and His intercession for you. You embrace His perfect intercession on your behalf and that of all the saints of God, and you rest assured that you acknowledge Him in all your ways. The Holy Spirit is guiding you and has worked out every possible direction you take for your good, all the while you fear and love God.

Please understand that this does not apply to the natural man who is not born again and only understands natural things. It does not even apply to the carnal Christian who is still focused on doing things according to the natural ways of men and the natural world, though this victorious Spirit-life is available to both. **I Corinthians 3:3**, as found in the Amplified Bible, provides a deeper understanding of those who operate carnally. It states, "For you are still [unspiritual, having the nature] of the flesh [under the control of ordinary impulses]. For as long as [there are] envying and jealousy and wrangling and factions among you, are you not unspiritual and of the flesh, behaving yourselves after a human standard and like mere (unchanged) men?"

Therefore, in order for every direction you take to be forward, you must be a Spirit-filled believer. **We have been placed on this earth as God's extension of mercy to reach the lives of those who do not know Him.** That is how great the love of God is for His creation, that even though they do not believe in Him, through us, the Body of Christ, He gives comfort, knowledge, and love to all with the hope that they too shall see Him through us. So that people will be brought out of the oppression of the enemy and enter into His rest.

To further understand this, the Word of God declares:

> And they had the hands of a man under their wings on their four sides; and they four had their faces and their wings. **Their wings were joined one to another; they turned not when they went; they went every one straight forward.** As for the likeness of their faces, they four had the face of a man, and the face of a lion, on the right side: and they four had the face of an ox on the left side; they four also had the face of an eagle. Thus were their faces: and their wings were stretched upward; two wings of every one were joined one to another, and two covered their bodies. **And they went every one straight forward: whither the spirit was to go, they went; and they turned not when they went. (Ezekiel 1:8-12)**

I used to read this portion of scripture above with the great mystery of these angelic beings, while all along, the images of these angels were God's message to humanity. God wants us to understand by the illumination of the Holy Spirit that He established these angels to show us how every direction and decision we make can be forward and in the Spirit.

First, He shows the hands of man under their wings, symbolizing that the works of man are to be divinely inspired and carried out with the power that is from above, and that the angels help us get the job done. **Next**, we observe that their wings are joined together, symbolizing that we are to work together in unity and in total agreement with God so that every direction is forward only as we are led by Him. **Finally**, He then goes to speak of the face of a man, lion, ox, and eagle, in which all have characteristics that speak of God's original design of man and woman being made in His image and likeness to love, rule, and dominate with power and vision on earth as it is in Heaven. Through Jesus Christ, all of this has been restored to us who believe in Him. We must embrace it and take action as we discover all He has done for us. The beauty of all this is that God has the Holy Spirit here and now to lead and guide us through all the Truth and discover as we go forth as co-laborers with Him to bring the whole world back to Him whom He so dearly loves.

Therefore, if we are led by the Spirit of God and hear Him tell us to take two steps forward, then we obey what He said; this is advancement for the Kingdom of God. No differently, if the Holy Spirit instructs us to hold our position or tells us to take a step backward, the advancement of the Kingdom still goes forth in that we heard and obeyed. So, every directive of the Holy Spirit that we obey advances the Kingdom of God regardless of our moving backward or forward. **The ultimate direction for us is obedience to whatever He commands, while the world is being directed back to Him as the Holy Spirit uses us to draw them to God.** This is why being led by the Holy Spirit is vital.

The unfortunate misconception of many in the body of Christ is that we must perform to obtain proof that we are sons of God in Christ Jesus. Let me assure you, the performer has declared it is finished. The one who produces and has already performed is God the Father in the Son Jesus Christ, whom we now abide in. Let Him who is in you do all the performance and give Him all the glory. He longs to show himself strong on your behalf and those around you. Please don't get caught up in the enemy's lies to make you think you have to do it to prove something to someone. Just point all to Jesus Christ and obey the Holy Spirit in all He instructs you to do, and before you know it, His performance in and through you will be evident for all to behold the one and only true living God! And He will get the glory, and we will all continually rejoice and be in awe of Him. Blessings to you all, in Jesus-Y'shua the Messiah's name, amen.

"Restoring Mankind's True Identity"

CHAPTER SEVEN

Repositioned out of Time into Eternity

Repositioned Out Of Time
Into Eternity

We have been repositioned out of time and into Eternity as believers. We must know where we have been "fitly" joined together in the Body of Christ so that we function correctly for the Glory of God. If we do not know our position, we will not function properly and will cause others not to operate to their fullest potential because we are out of place. The good news is that if you are born again, <u>God has brought you out of time and birthed you into Eternity, as He calls you His child.</u> Meditate on that statement. Before I get ahead of myself, let us see the definitions of **Time** and **Eternity**.

Time – two types of time in the Greek Strong Concordance: *Kairos* and *Chronos*.

> #2540 Greek word (**Kairos**) – means a set or proper time, such as a season, opportunity, due time, always a season, a time, a period, a favorable opportunity, time as it brings forth several events. A fixed or special occasion marked by certain features.

An example of this would be you sow in spring; then you reap the harvest as you water the seed sown through the season in which it can grow and produce for the harvesting season.

> #5550 Greek word (**Chronos**) – means simply time, as such of, or the succession of moment's together, length. A space of time whether long or short; it implies duration such as 24 hours in a day etc. It sometimes refers to the date of an occurrence, whether past or future.

God the Father in **Acts 1:17** has set within His own Authority both the times *Chronos*, the length of the periods, and the season *Kairos*. It is essential to understand that God has authority over time, and He is not subject to time, whether *Chronos* or *Karios*, as He is the Eternal One, Self-Existing One. The Word of God declares in **II Peter 3:8,** *"But, beloved, be not ignorant of this one thing, that one day is with the Lord as a thousand years, and a thousand years as one day."* God operates from Eternity into time. He brings forth what to Him already is, as He finished it all from and before the foundation of the earth. Remember, God rested on the seventh day because He finished His work.

Now that we understand God has authority over all time, let's look at the word Eternity. **Eternity** in Hebrew Strong #5710 means *duration, in the sense of perpetuity, everlasting, more, world without end.* So simply stated, it means everlasting, perpetual, forever, and ever without end.

Further, in this natural world, mankind abides in natural time, a measured time (*Chronos*), and an opportune time (*Kairos*). Time exists for every person in a body in this world. As believers in Christ Jesus, we have been repositioned. We have been brought out of *Chronos* time and out of *Kairos* time. We have been placed and birthed into Eternity. We abide in the Eternal One as we are members of the Body of Jesus Christ, the King of kings and Lord of lords. God purposely brought us out of time and placed us into eternity to now operate from eternity into natural time. So, as we abide in the Eternal One, He has set us up to rule and reign on the Earth in Jesus' name. God set us up for victory, not defeat; He set us up for the best, not the worst, for we must know how to follow Jesus, the Messiah whom God sent.

We are followers of Jesus the Messiah, His disciples. If that is true for the believer, we must examine how we are speaking, conducting ourselves, and reverencing Him. We must examine and see if we are obeying God as Jesus did while on earth. Remember, we should be doing what Jesus did. If we follow Jesus, we ought to know what our destiny holds for us because He knew for what purpose and end He was sent into this world. As children, we hear we can become anything we want, which is true because we have been given free will. However, if we genuinely seek God and His Kingdom, we must first find our intimate relationship with Him. We must also know why He has sent us into this world, and in knowing this, we will know what He has originally designed for us to be. Decide today to truly live out in this world what He desires so that starting now, we may reap the benefits of the world that is to come (**Hebrews 6:4-5**).

Life in God should never take us by surprise regarding our purpose. No believer should be living day by day. Take a look at what today brings the believer. A believer lives by faith on purpose all the time. Remember what **Romans 1:17** says, "*The Just Shall Live by Faith,*" and as God brought us who believe in Him out of time and placed us in eternity so that we could now by Him function in natural time—we are to hear His voice and know how to follow His plan for our lives here on earth. As we hear and obey Him, we will see good success.

Moreover, we will now look at **Luke Chapter 19, verses 1 through 10**, to see the process of how this takes place; to see how one is positioned because of God's goodness, how He sends forth His Word in the midst of the warfare of life, and to see how He must abide with those who receive Jesus Christ whom He has sent.

Luke 19:1
"And Jesus entered and passed through Jericho."

Jesus, the Living Word, was made flesh and passed through Jericho. He enters into the zone of your warfare (**Joshua 4:13**); in this place, impossibilities can only be overcome by God and man/woman obeying and relying solely on God to get him/her the VICTORY. However, the enemy continually deceives humanity into thinking that the fight is theirs to figure out and conquer by their own strength. God has already defeated the enemy and is waiting for His people to obey Him so that He may give them victory as they follow His instructions. The leaders, along with the people, must trust God for the fullness of the Promised Land to come to pass visibly for each member of the Body of Christ Jesus.

To accomplish this victory, one must reject the evil heart of unbelief and embrace in faith that which God has already won for us in Christ Jesus.

Hebrews 3:12
"Take heed, brethren, lest there be in any of you an evil heart of unbelief, in departing from the Living God."

Hebrews 3:19
"So we see that they could not enter into the Promised Land because of unbelief."

Unbelief will keep you from the best life God has provided for you. In the Old Testament, those who came out of Egypt with Moses could not enter the promised land because of their unbelief, but those who believed entered and won.

Remember Joshua and the wall of Jericho: God had Joshua circumcise the men of Israel days before they would have to face the enemy and the walls of Jericho. God, through His covenant, would deliver the victory into their hands. I am here to declare to you that Jesus has delivered all enemies into your hands! **ONLY BELIEVE!** Obey the Lord and shout when He tells you to shout. Praise Him, for He fights for you!

Joshua 6:16
"And it came to pass at the seventh time, when the priests blew with the trumpets, Joshua said unto the people, Shout; for the LORD hath given you the city."

The Living Word is passing by your place of warfare right now, whether sickness, pandemics, poverty, unemployment, family trouble, or your marriage—He has declared you a VICTOR and not a victim. So, if you believe the Word of the Lord, take some time to shout big praises to Him! Celebrate the Lord this day, for He has given you the VICTORY.

Do you believe that? If you do, glorify Jesus this day and every day. As you do, you will see that, as the Lord was with Joshua, He is with you and will cause all to know that you have a covenant with Almighty God.

Joshua 6:27
"So the LORD was with Joshua; and his fame was noised throughout all the country."

Saints of God, as you obey and unite under the authority of the Word of God, it will be known throughout the country that God is with you, and He brings forth the victory continuously as you believe. The Lord is with you because you abide in Jesus the Messiah. HalleluYah!

The next verse in the Bible:

Luke 19:2
"And, behold, there was a man named Zacchaeus, which was the chief among the publicans, and he was rich."

Behold, there was a man named **Zacchaeus, which means PURE, TRANSPARENT, CLEAN**. He was a chief among the tax gatherers for the world system, and he was rich. But, unfortunately, the man who was to be clean, transparent, and pure was in the wrong system, as many men and women are today in the world, robbing and becoming rich by unjust gain, totally out of position in God's divine plan for them. Zacchaeus was a chief and rich in a system designed to exploit and demand hard labor from others under a cursed system.

The ignorance of humanity deceived by a fallen system leads them to think they have to work the system and put hard labor on others to get rich, but all along, the Lord is saying, *"The Battle is not yours. It is Mine."*

> "And he said, Hearken ye, all Judah, and ye inhabitants of Jerusalem, and thou king Jehoshaphat, Thus saith the LORD unto you, **Be not afraid nor dismayed by reason of this great multitude; for the battle is not yours, but God's.** Tomorrow go ye down against them: behold, they come up by the cliff of Ziz; and ye shall find them at the end of the brook, before the wilderness of Jeruel. Ye shall not need to fight in this battle: set yourselves, stand ye still, and see the salvation of the Lord with you, O Judah and Jerusalem: fear not, nor be dismayed; tomorrow go out against them: for the LORD will be with you. And Jehoshaphat bowed his head with his face to the ground: and all Judah and the inhabitants of Jerusalem fell before the LORD, worshipping the LORD. **(II Chronicles 20:15-18)**

Therefore, as we worship the Lord Jesus, "Y'shua," the Messiah, He reminds us as He declared unto us, *"IT IS FINISHED!"* On the Cross, Jesus Christ declared this and gave up the Ghost **(see John 19:30)**.

The next verse in the Bible:

Luke 19:3
"And he sought to see Jesus who he was; and could not for the press, because he was little of stature."

This man in a fallen system, Zacchaeus, who was to be Clean, Pure, and Transparent, sought to see the Living Word made Flesh. **Acts 13:48,** *"And when the Gentiles heard this, they were glad, and glorified the word of the Lord: and as* *many as were ordained to eternal life believed."* When men hear good news, they are drawn to it and want to see it for themselves. However, this man could not get to **the Living Word**, "Jesus," because of the multitudes of people. The same happens today: Such stumbling blocks exist that Satan put up to keep humanity from receiving the Word of God-made Flesh. These stumbling blocks can be the religion of men, gossip, jealousy, and judging. It is any challenge or obstacle of the enemy to keep people from knowing the Truth of God and the Messiah whom God sent. Satan knows if you find out the Truth that you are going to be brought out of the natural world and its time and translated into Eternity to then function back in time by God in you, which will whip the devil again and again.

Zacchaeus was a SMALL man; he could not see, but that did not stop him. The people who have yet to encounter the Living Word of God do not have to settle for slavery, sickness, depression, and all that the system of the world governed by Satan offers. **They can climb up like Zacchaeus!**

Many times, people who think of themselves as small desire places of authority to show others their value and worth. Their battle is an internal one. Many times, people who are immature in the things of God have yet to renew their minds to the Word of God and bring in the system of the world to the local congregation because they want to be seen, but in reality, God sees you. Seek Him, and He will take care of the rest and reposition you to where He wants you to be, for He has ordained you to be for His Glory.

Taking Action to See the Word Made Flesh

Luke 19:4
"And he ran before, and climbed up into a sycamore tree to see him: for he was to pass that way."

Zacchaeus, the pure, transparent, clean man, ran **before to climb.** Let me tell you that you must run, take action, and climb in prayer and in the Word of God in order to see the Word made flesh and for you to receive it with joy. **You must labor in the Word and believe to receive Heaven's best.** You know God is present and has already done everything for us. Now, you must believe by faith because He is passing your way all the time in your time of warfare, for He is always present. Therefore, as the Word of God comes forth, **it is an opportune time, a Kairos Time,** for you to receive by faith His best for your life.

This is an opportune time to come out of natural time and be born into Eternity because of Jesus Christ, our Lord. This is available to you now, **THIS DAY!** This day, you become one with Eternity as a member in the Body of Christ to manifest in natural time the will of God on Earth as it is in Heaven.

Luke 19:5
"And when Jesus came to the place, he looked up, and saw him, and said unto him, Zacchaeus, make haste, and come down; for today I must abide at thy house."

When you believe, God notices! The Word made Flesh comes and manifests Himself to you and declares as you BELIEVE, "*I must abide with you*" because God made a covenant with Abraham, and you are a son of Abraham. Now you pass from mortal to Eternal Life because you believe. **STOP WAITING FOR ETERNITY. YOU HAVE ETERNAL LIFE NOW IF YOU BELIEVE!** The Word of God declares in John

17:3, *"And **this is life eternal,** that they might know thee the only true God, and Jesus Christ, whom thou hast sent."* If you know Jesus Christ as your Lord and Savior, you have eternal life right now. Summarizing **John 1:1-3**, *"In the beginning was the Word and Word was with God, and the Word was God, and He made all things."* The fantastic news is that through Jesus Christ and the dispensation of Grace we are in, the believer, through faith in love, has been made a member of Eternity in Christ Jesus. We are seated in Heavenly places in Him, and as He is, so are we in this world (see **I John 4:17**).

We are partakers of the powers of the world to come now.

> For it is impossible for those who were once enlightened, and have tasted of the heavenly gift, and were made partakers of the Holy Ghost, And have tasted the good word of God, and the powers of the world to come. (**Hebrews 6:4-5**)

As born-again believers, we have been taken out of natural time and birthed into Eternity. **II Corinthians 5:17** tells how we are of a **new nature—one with Christ. Romans 8:17** states that we are joint heirs with Jesus Christ, while **I Corinthians 6:17** says that we are of one Spirit with the Lord. Thus, being able to declare as Jesus declared, I and my Father are one in Christ Jesus.

Furthermore, Jesus said in **John 10:30,** *"I and my Father are one."* As we awaken to this, for which God has called and made us, we hear and follow in Jesus' footsteps and do what He did and do even greater works in his name.

> My sheep hear my voice, and I know them, and they follow me: **And I give unto them eternal life; and they shall never perish, neither shall any man pluck them out of my hand.** My Father, which gave them me, is greater than all; and no man is able to

pluck them out of my Father's hand. I and my Father are one. **(John 10:27-30)**

But we have this treasure in earthen vessels, that the Excellency of the power may be of God, and not of us. (II Corinthians 4:7)

While we look not at the things which are seen, but at the things which are not seen: for the things which are seen are temporal; but the things which are not seen are eternal. **(II Corinthians 4:18)**

Our bodies are the temple of the Holy Spirit of God. He abides in us, and the Excellency of power comes from God into this world through believers who are vessels surrendered to Him. As we yield to Him, He gives us an understanding of our position in Him, leading us to stop focusing on ourselves and on this natural, visible world. He leads us to see the eternal purpose. This is what we must bring forth as manifested sons of His in Christ Jesus.

We are operating in Christ Jesus from Eternity into Natural time. This brings great understanding into how Jesus operated, seeing only what the Father did and speaking only what the Father Spoke.

Therefore the Jews sought the more to kill him, because he not only had broken the sabbath, but said also that God was his Father, making himself equal with God. 19 Then answered Jesus and said unto them, Verily, verily, I say unto you, The Son can do nothing of himself, but what he seeth the Father do: for what things soever he doeth, these also doeth the Son likewise. **(John 5:18-19)**

Do we declare God is our Father? Yes! Then what we are saying is that through Christ, we have, by Jesus' merits, been made equal with God as we abide in Christ and, therefore, would be accused in the exact same manner the Jews accused Jesus. **Notice again that the Son does nothing of Himself except what He sees the FATHER DO.**

In **Luke 19:6**, it says, *"And he made haste, and came down, and received him joyfully."* In order to operate this way, we must first do what Zacchaeus did, which was to position himself and make haste to receive the Word joyfully and wholeheartedly by taking action to become one with the Word. By coming to the Word, embracing the Word, and believing the Word, the Word will Manifest and bring forth CONVICTION OF SIN, and as We Repent, the Manifestation and Presence of God's Word will be made visible to all!

Next, **Luke 19:7** states, *"And when they saw it, they all murmured, saying, That he was gone to be guest with a man that is a sinner."* Notice that the Living Word is no respecter of persons; this man was a sinner, but as this man repented, the Living Word went home with him. Others murmured how the Living Word could go with Zacchaeus, the sinner, forgetting their own faults and sins before a Holy God. They also needed to repent and be positioned in their rightful place to be in unity with God as One to serve and save others, and not condemn them.

Also, in **Luke 19:8**, *"And Zacchaeus stood, and said unto the Lord: Behold, Lord, the half of my goods I give to the poor; and if I have taken anything from any man by false accusation, I restore him fourfold."* When a man is convicted of sin and has true repentance, he becomes totally transparent and clean. He joyfully submits to the good news of the Word of God and desires to make right any wrong he may have committed if he can. Then, he runs to ask for forgiveness and bless those around him. A person does this because the True Gospel of God is the best wine.

Wine can symbolize life in the Bible, so you can say that the true Good News of God is the best Life that exists!

Once a person receives the Good News of God, they will gladly repent, **have a change of mind**, and trust God, but first, they must have true repentance and a true belief.

There have been times when people have tried faith in God and tried believing, but there is no such thing. Either you truly believe and have faith, or you have none. The Word of God declares in **Deuteronomy 4:29**, "*But if from thence thou shalt seek the Lord thy God, thou shalt find him, if thou seek him with all thy heart and with all thy soul.*" And in **Jeremiah 29:13**, "*And ye shall seek me, and find me, when ye shall search for me with all your heart.*" Nevertheless, the people who have tried to live for God never truly have repented from the heart, for the Word of God declares that when you turn to God with all your heart and seek Him, you will find Him, and He will make Himself known to you.

This Day

The Living Word, Jesus, answers those who repent and declares, this day, not tomorrow, not in the past or the future, but **THIS DAY, SALVATION HAS COME TO THIS HOUSE!** Zacchaeus heard this in **Luke 19:9**, "*And Jesus said unto him, This day is salvation come to this house, forsomuch as he also is a son of Abraham.*" If you embrace Jesus, the outcome of your embrace of Him will be salvation for your house. Jesus "Y'shua" is the Lord of all, and He has declared that **this day is the day of Salvation, Restoration, Healing, Victory, Deliverance, Prosperity, Holiness, and Righteousness with God. This day is the day of REST and the day of your Jubilee**, for Jesus is the Lord of all who has overridden time by His faith to manifest Himself to you the goodwill of God toward all who believe in Him. HalleluYah!

Leviticus 25 talks about the Day of Rest and the Year of Jubilee, a day when you do not have to toil and sweat but enjoy the provision of God. A time of Jubilee and total Restoration of all that was lost, of every wrong decision you made that caused you loss, restored. The Lord of All is declaring by the Holy Spirit,

> **STOP WAITING, YOU HAVE ETERNITY NOW BECAUSE YOU HAVE ME! NOW GO AND BRING FORTH LIFE WHEREVER YOU GO IN MY NAME AND MAKE OF ALL TIME AN OPPORTUNE TIME AS YOU LIVE AND WALK BY FAITH, BRINGING THE WILL OF THE KINGDOM OF GOD ON EARTH AS IT IS IN HEAVEN.**

When a person chooses to believe in Jesus the Messiah, that person becomes a son or daughter of Abraham and now has God's covenant with them. So the Covenant of God and all its benefits are with all who have faith in Him through Jesus the Messiah.

It truly is finished! It is already done. Only believe and know who it is that God has made you. Think about it: God did not withhold His Only Begotten Son to pay the price for your whole being. He has placed value in each one of us far beyond the worth of anything that exists in any visible or invisible realm. It is time to stop fighting among each other and start building together for the Glory of God, as we allow unity to be based upon what God has declared in His Word, the new and better Covenant. **GOD HAS MADE US MANIFESTATIONS OF HIS KINGDOM UPON THE EARTH.**

Finally, in **Luke 19:10**, the Word of God declares, *"For the Son of man is come to seek and to save that which was lost."* For the Son of Man, made in the image and likeness of God, comes to seek and to save, not condemn nor judge. Jesus did not come to cause people to perish, but to save, bless, give victory, prosper, and make holy those lost. In **I Peter 3:22**, it says Jesus is in Heaven and is at the right hand of God, and all angels, authorities, and powers are made subject unto Him.

The word of God teaches us in **Ephesians 2:6** that we are seated with Jesus, and as we abide in Him and are in the Spirit, these angels, authorities, and powers are made subject unto us in His name upon the earth, as they are to Him in Heaven.

Do you serve Jesus? If yes, then you follow Jesus, and where Jesus is, so are you. **John 12:26** Jesus Christ said, *"If any man serve me, let him follow me; and where I am, there shall also my servant be: if any man serve me, him will my Father honour."* The Father honors us as He honors Jesus because we serve Him. Praise God! Knowing that where Jesus is, so are we, because we have been born of God's Spirit, we have been born into Eternity. We can now come out of natural time and into Eternity as we operate by the Spirit of God.

How is it possible that God's goodwill can be toward all men? **Luke 2:14** *"Glory to God in the highest, and on earth peace, good will toward men."* Because of Jesus and the perfect work of His sacrifice on the cross for humanity. Believers in Christ are now His Body upon the earth to bring forth by His Holy Spirit His goodwill toward all mankind.

As believers, we operate from Eternity into natural time as manifested sons of God upon the earth. We are the portals in which God visibly makes Himself known to all mankind, as we died with Christ and rose with Him in Spirit as we believe in Him. We die to ourselves in the area of the soul that needs to be renewed to the new reality of being born of God's Spirit. We co-labor with the Holy Spirit to have His way through us in Jesus "Y'shua's" name that His beauty is made known by us. Amen!

We are children of Eternity operating in natural time as sons and daughters of God. Therefore, we must master stepping out of natural time and into Eternity to take from Eternity the provision and solutions of the Kingdom of God and bring forth the will of God in this natural time world. The objective of this is to draw humanity back toward God through His net of Grace in Christ Jesus, given to us who believe. As sons and daughters of God, we are the manifestations of God upon the earth if we live in the Spirit. This is why Jesus said if you have seen Me, you have seen the Father.

> Jesus saith unto him, Have I been so long time with you, and yet hast thou not known me, Philip? **he that hath seen me hath seen the Father; and how sayest thou then, Show us the Father? Believest thou not that I am in the Father, and the Father in me?** the words that I speak unto you I speak not of myself: but the Father that dwelleth in me, he doeth the works. (**John 14:9-10**)

Where Jesus is, I am as a believer in the Spirit: Where God is by Grace in Christ Jesus, I am as a believer who lives in the Spirit. We must come to the place where we say, as Jesus, whom we follow, "he that hath seen me hath seen the Father," because we are members of the body of Christ Jesus.

We are Ambassadors, agents in Eternity operating in natural time by the faith of the Son of God.

> I am crucified with Christ: nevertheless I live; yet not I, but Christ liveth in me: and the life which I now live in the flesh I live by the faith of the Son of God, who loved me, and gave himself for me. (**Galatians 2:20**)

The moment we are born of the Spirit, we are born into Eternity because the Spirit is Eternal. We must know that by Grace, the way God the Father endorses and honors Jesus, He endorses and honors us as born-again believers—there is nothing we cannot do with God. God is for us (see **Romans 8:31-32 and John 12:26**). Our lives should never happen by accident as sons of God.

As Jesus knew His destiny and mission, so can you and I as we commune and have intimate fellowship with God.

> And Jesus answered and said, Verily I say unto you, There is no man that hath left house, or brethren, or sisters, or father, or mother, or wife, or children, or lands, for my sake, and the gospel's, But he shall receive an hundredfold now in this time, houses, and brethren, and sisters, and mothers, and children, and lands, with persecutions; and in the world to come eternal life. But many that are first shall be last; and the last first. And they were in the way going up to Jerusalem; and Jesus went before them: and they were amazed; and as they followed, they were afraid. **And he took again the twelve, and began to tell them what things should happen unto him, Saying, Behold, we go up to Jerusalem; and the Son of man shall be delivered unto the chief priests, and unto the scribes; and they shall condemn him to death, and shall deliver him to the Gentiles: And they shall mock him, and shall scourge him, and shall spit upon him, and shall kill him: and the third day he shall rise again. (Mark 10:29-34 KJV)**

Every believer in Christ can hear God and know their purpose. As you operate from Eternity into natural time, you operate with the powers that are from Eternity. Therefore, you are able to override time, whether it is Chronos or Kairos time. Jesus said in **John 4:35** *"Say not ye, There are yet four months, and then cometh harvest? behold, I say unto you, Lift up your eyes, and look on the fields; for they are white already to harvest."* Say not four months, and then the harvest. The harvest is READY NOW! Faith says NOW THIS IS THE DAY!

We must operate from the Spirit, the Eternal, into this natural time world by faith in order to get instant results as God the Father instructs us to do. **John 6:53-63** shows Jesus speaking the language of the Spirit, for the Spirit has its own language. Jesus said, "***You must eat of my Flesh and drink of my Blood.***" He was speaking Spirit, saying His meat is the will of God; His Word made flesh for all to live and not die. Jesus' Blood is the new and true testament, as well as the new wine that is available to drink and distribute so that no one is left thirsty but is fully supplied with the abundance of life. The new wine of life gave us victory over all darkness and brought forth healing, prosperity, holiness, and provisions of God. This is now in you and me to give to others. Remember in **II Peter 3:8** that to God, one day is as a thousand, and a thousand is as one day. Why? Because He lives and is the Eternal One, the Self-Existing One—always has been, always will be, and Jesus is the Alpha and Omega, the Beginning and the End.

Now, as we know the Truth, the love of God is the love of the believer because His Spirit is one with ours. This also applies to God's Faith, Wisdom, Grace, Mercy, Joy, Prosperity, Victory, and all other things of God. HalleluYah! Jesus has returned humanity that repents of sin back to our rightful place as people who are made in the image and likeness of God in Him.

The Future

It is common knowledge that technology is advancing on levels that humanity has never experienced before in the twenty-first century. Breakthroughs in bioengineering, biomimicry, cyborg engineering, artificial intelligence, and many other technological fields introduce societies to live in ways that seemed like fantasy a couple of centuries ago. Nevertheless, Jesus Christ dominated these areas in ways beyond human reason: For example, He multiplied two fish and five loaves of bread and fed over five thousand people in a matter of minutes (**Mark 6:37-44**), far beyond bioengineering capabilities. Concerning Biomimicry, God introduced the thought "consider the ant" (see Proverbs 6:6) concerning cyborg engineering to give people new limbs if they lost an arm or a leg. Jesus Christ made the maimed whole (see **Matthew 15:31**).

Further, if humanity ever discovers how to teleport objects or people in any way, Jesus Christ did that long before on many occasions (see **John 6:19-27 and Acts 8:39-40**). Humanity is exploring space and has designed plans to leave the Earth if necessary due to its fear of global warming and lack of resources. Some scientists believe that the Earth will run out of supplies, and climate change will cause the Earth to become uninhabitable at some point. Despite all technological advances, they are simply discovering what God the Creator has placed on the earth to be discovered in the visible and invisible realms.

Perhaps instead of being driven by fear, humanity should focus on the fact that the Creator of all that is being discovered is more than enough to continue to provide the earth's resources for humans to live. Furthermore, if there were a need for a new Earth, God is more than able to provide it when the time comes. What is surprising is that everything discovered in one form or another, God has introduced to humanity through His Word. It seems like the world without God goes about as the sorcerers in the time of Pharaoh. When Moses threw the staff on the ground, it became a serpent, and the magicians of Pharaoh did the same; they went on with turning water into blood and bringing forth frogs upon the land of Egypt (**Exodus Chapters 7 and 8**). However, when the Lord brought forth lice and other plagues against Pharaoh, his magicians could not replicate what the Lord, the Creator, did. Similarly, some people have made it their mission to extend human life and dream of the day they can defeat death.

Nevertheless, what these people who seek to defeat death

by way of science and other highly educated atheists fail to understand is that even if they managed to extend human life to thousands of years, they would only be addressing the external matter and not the internal one that allows humanity to think and be uniquely and wonderfully made. Humanity's soul is eternal, and the condition of each individual's soul can only be saved through being born again through Jesus Christ, the Word of God made flesh. There are many people in the world today who have everything they could possibly dream of concerning this natural material world, yet it is undeniable that there are invisible forces at work all around the visible experience that every human life lives. Due to this mystery of the invisible forces, humanity without God seeks ways to solve the problems that are beyond their understanding, and they go around in circles, making up many hypotheses and theories that lead to many roads built on foundations that are not solid, and only add more distortion and confusion to humanity.

In the end, without God, humanity will continue to create many paths that lead to emptiness and the void of God's true intent for each person's life. Therefore, the wisest thing an individual can do is seek God, who created all the beautiful things that are seen and the mysteries of the unseen, to ensure a life worth living to the glory of the Creator. God is He who, from what the world calls nothing, makes all things. He is beyond time, for He is the Eternal One who created time beyond the mysteries of the Universe and all the known and unknown galaxies. Therefore, God is the only definition of Absolute Truth (**John 14:6, John 17:17, 1 John 4:5-6, and Romans 3:4**), for He is in a class of His own without his creation. Still, God invites all humans to be restored to their rightful image and likeness and be made sons and daughters of God in Christ Jesus, the Word of God made flesh for all humankind to be graced to be heirs of God and joint-heirs with Christ.

A s we do Truth, we are one with Truth!

Confession of Faith

Confess: God, your Love is my love, your Faith is my faith, Your Hope is my hope, Your Wisdom is my wisdom, Your Strength is my strength, Your Riches are my riches, and all You are and have you have given me in Christ Jesus, Y'shua the Messiah. This day, I take my rightful place and position that You have graced me to have, and I am in expectancy that as You confirmed Joshua to the people of Israel, now You confirm me from this day forward, privately and publicly, that You are my God and You are for me. Thank you, God, in Jesus' name, I act now by faith to take the Gospel of the Kingdom of Heaven in every place You lead me to for Your glory in Your divine will for this body, which is now Your temple. Amen.

Joshua 3:7, *"And the LORD said unto Joshua, This day will I begin to magnify thee in the sight of all Israel, that they may know that, as I was with Moses, so I will be with thee."*

Remember, there is only one Truth, so we of the Truth imitate and do as Truth does. There is only one Author of the Truth, God! All others are to abide and imitate, and do as we see Truth do (**Ephesians 5:1**). Those who do not believe in God do not believe in Truth (**1 John 4:5-6**), **for the only definition of Absolute Truth that exists is God**. Meditate and think on this revelation.

Now go, my beloved brothers and sisters, be aware of your new identity in the Glory of God. Expect manifestations of the Word of God and be doers of it as it has been sown into your being, that you may bear good fruit unto God the Father in the name of Y'shua—Jesus Christ. Amen! Your brother in Christ, Geovanni Israel Guerra.

Empowering Daily Confession

Because I am born of God, by Grace, through faith, rooted in love, in Y'shua—Jesus the Messiah's name, I NOW HAVE OVERCOME THE WORLD because of the faith in me and the one of whom I am now one with, in Spirit and in Truth. I have a new and better covenant, in which God has sworn: He would not be angry with me, so I am free from all condemnation and accusations, and now partake of the divine new nature, which is of God in Spirit and in Truth. I have been bought with the Blood of Jesus Christ. Therefore, I belong to Him; my soul is not mine, but it is His soul in me as I was crucified with Christ. I now live by His Faith. I am a manifested mature child of God, in whom Jesus was the first among many. I believe in Him as the Son of God. My Heavenly Father not only knows what I need, but He also grants me my heart's desires, for my delight is in Him. I am blessed with the blessing of Abraham, and God has made me a blessing to all the families of the earth. As He has blessed me and made me a great nation, the uttermost parts of the earth are already in my possession. My High Priest Y'shua—Jesus has said of me, BLESSED BE (put your name here) and my family of the Most High God El Elyon, possessors of Heaven and earth and blessed be the Most High God who has given us all our enemies into our hands and of all things I bring whatsoever the Lord request, the minimum the tithe. I owe no man anything but to love them, and I receive Heaven's best daily, and this day is no exception! God has been mindful of me because I believe in Him and His Word, as it multiplies me daily with Heaven's Best increase. God had Jesus, the Lamb of God, His only begotten Son, to be made sin for me, suffering the penalty of my sins. Therefore, I boldly declare: I am the righteousness of God, and I rule and reign in this life by one Jesus Christ—Y'shua Adonai! No weapon formed against me will ever prosper, and any tongue that rises up against me in judgment, I condemn, for my righteousness is of the Lord. The favor of God rests richly upon me as a believer in Christ

Jesus, and God fights against those who fight against me, and He has saved my children. THE BLESSING OF THE LORD has made me rich in every area of my life, spirit, soul, body, and financially, and it has no toil or sweat with it. The abundant life is manifesting in my life, and the blessings of the Lord are continually overtaking me. A shield of favor is around my life, spouse, children, and anyone God assigns me for His Glory in Jesus' name. I am the head and not the tail. I am blessed in the city and in the field when I go and when I come. All evil, viruses, sicknesses, diseases, lack, poverty, depression, oppression, unbelief, doubt, misfortune, disunity, strife, stress, frustration, fear, shame, perversion, terror, rejection, and rebellion are far from my life and homes in Jesus' name. I decree health, wealth, the abundance of love, life, prosperity, grace, peace, and joy in the Holy Ghost abounding in me and flowing out of me everywhere I go as a believer in Jesus the Messiah and upon everything I do. I forget none of the benefits of the Lord-He has healed all my diseases and has imputed unto me that which Jesus has made to be my portion, which is Wisdom, Riches, Honor, Power, Strength, Glory, and Blessing, and where He is, I am as His servant and mature offspring. I am the light of the world. I am the salt of the earth from above and not from beneath, and so is every member of the body of Christ, because God said so! I decree: as a believer, I lay up gold as dust, wealth, and riches are in my home for my life and all generations to come upon my children and children's children until the trumpet sounds and Jesus comes in the clouds. I decree: the Spirit of wisdom and understanding of God is upon me, and I live after and in the Spirit and mortify the deeds of the flesh daily. Whatever I say as a believer are words of Spirit and life, and as I have been made one Spirit with the Lord and have the mind of Christ, I think with His mind and mindset, and His command is my manifestation upon the earth in Jesus' name! For those of us who are married, our matrimony and family are held in the palm of God's right hand, and He keeps us. We only speak what we hear the Father speak, and no word we speak in the Spirit will fall to the ground! Whatever we touch prospers and is gold for God's Glory. As a believer, I fear the Lord and He alone! My life, spouse, and children are olive trees planted by the rivers of living water that bear good fruit in season and out of season. My household and I are the redeemed of the Lord, and we say so! We are one with the God kind of faith, and the kingdom of God manifests daily through us. We are dispellers of darkness! We are giant slayers, anointed and appointed to resolve, rebuild, and restore! Wisdom, understanding, and revelation knowledge of God are that which we operate by through the Holy Spirit of God with us, in us, and upon us with power in Jesus' name! We cast out devils, we speak new tongues, we tread on serpents and scorpions, and nothing by any means shall hurt us. We lay hands on the sick, and they recover, in Jesus' name! We are ministers of Grace and speak to build, exhort, and comfort. The anointing and fire of the Holy Ghost is breaking every yoke and removing every burden everywhere we go, in Jesus' name! God rebukes the devourer on our behalf. We have open windows of Heaven blessing upon us through faith by Grace as we believe in the Lord. All nations call us blessed everywhere we go, for God Almighty has made us a delightsome land. We are on fire for God, and the flame of the Spirit of God will never diminish in us as the Body of Christ but grows and lights up the world in Jesus— Y"shua's name. My family and all those connected to me are the healed of the Most High God in Y'shua—Jesus' name, Amen!

When I Look in the Mirror: Confession

When I look into the true mirror, which reflects who God has made me, I see God the Father, the Son, and the Holy Spirit who indwell me. I see a manifested son of God upon the earth, ruling and reigning in Jesus' name. I see the Power of God in demonstration without limits, the Wisdom of God, the Love of God, and the Word made Flesh. I see the Kingdom of God dominating in and through me, in Jesus' name! I see the

Faith of God and the fullness of his unlimited expression through this, his earthly vessel. I see joy, peace, patience, long-suffering, meekness, kindness, and gentleness. I see resurrection power giving life to those who are hopeless around me. I see the glory cloud of the Lord upon me and everywhere I stand, full of life and God's goodness! I see the Holiness of God, the righteousness of God, and the beauty of God. When I look into the mirror, I see the Favor of God, the Blessing of God, and all his riches upon me to meet every need in Jesus' name so that He may get the glory. I see the Lord's healing virtue flowing out of me, healing the nations with the Gospel of the Kingdom of God in Jesus' name. This is what God sees; therefore, it is what I see of myself now and forever in Jesus' name, amen!

1 John 3:2 Beloved, now are we the sons of God, and it doth not yet appear what we shall be: but we know that, when he shall appear, we shall be like him; for we shall see him as he is.

James 1:23-25 23 For if any be a hearer of the word, and not a doer, he is like unto a man beholding his natural face in a glass: 24 For he beholdeth himself, and goeth his way, and straightway forgetteth what manner of man he was. 25 But whoso looketh into the perfect law of liberty, and continueth therein, he being not a forgetful hearer, but a doer of the work, this man shall be blessed in his deed.

A Prayer to Pray

Abba, Father, I cast my soul (mind, will, and emotions, which include my intellect and imagination) on you to have it process and produce only from the life of your Spirit in me. Guard against all information and areas of my soul that were not taught by you, and root them out. Have your complete expression and process through my soul with your Holy Spirit as the only influential source upon me and manifest your will from the Spirit into this natural realm, by this your temple, my body, into this world, in Jesus' name. You keep me, and as You have instructed me to accept and receive what You do for me, I pray according to Your Word in **Mark 11:23-24**, believing that I have received my petitions according to Your Word and in faith know I have them, in Jesus' name. I have it now; it is unto me as you have spoken in Jesus' name, Amen!

Thank you for reading my book. I truly hope it has blessed you and that you will give it a review at overcomingtheworldpublishing.com. The website will take you directly to my Amazon author page, where you can click on the book, scroll down, and click "**write a customer review.**" I highly value your remarks, and it would be a blessing to hear what God has done with this book to empower the body of Christ. Thank you in advance, and may God bless you in Jesus' name, amen.

Sincerely,

Geovanni I. Guerra

Order the following books in the series *of*

Think and Speak Like God Restoring Mankind's True Identity:

What do you see in the Mirror? Mirror, Mirror, Flesh or Spirit?

The Mindset of Christ.

The Mother of Jesus: Not Just Mary.

In Spanish-Español

Piensa y Habla Como Dios: Restaurando La Verdadera Identidad del Ser Humano.

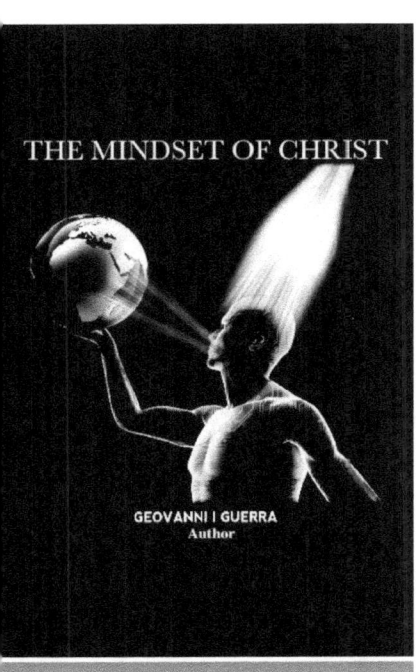

THE MINDSET OF CHRIST

GEOVANNI I GUERRA
Author

O.T.W.
PUBLISHING INC.

What Do You See
In The Mirror?

Inspired & Forward by Holy Spirit.

Geovanni Israel Guerra

*Order your copies online;
available at Amazon, BAM,
Barnes & Noble, and
Walmart.*

Notes

Notes

Notes

Notes

Notes

www.ingramcontent.com/pod-product-compliance
Lightning Source LLC
Chambersburg PA
CBHW071355120626
46546CB00002B/699